Make the Best of the Rest of your Life

To Adam ~
You are fabulous !!
What a joy to meet you.
Geri O'Neill

facim.org

Disappearance of the Universe

www.gerioneill.com

New and Expanded Edition

This book is for entertainment and educational purposes only.
It is not for use in the treatment of medical or psychological conditions.
If you need specific advise see your health professional.

Make the Best of the Rest of Your Life
Copyright © Geri O'Neill 2008.

ISBN: 978 0 9804896 6 1 3

Inkstone Press, Australia
www.inkstone-press.com

Printed in Malaysia

Make the Best of the Rest of your Life

Inspiring

Entertaining

Thought-Provoking

Informative

Geri O'Neill

inkstone

For my mother, Nancy O'Neill
Who blessed my life with love and laughter
1918 - 2006

CONTENTS

At any moment I could start
being more of the person I dream to be...
But which moment should I choose?

Ashleigh Brilliant

Chapter 1

JUMPING OFF THE CLIFF

The important thing is this:
To be able at any moment to
sacrifice what we are
for what we could become.

Charles DuBois

You are never too young or too old to change. Change is a magic wand we all possess. You can change your brain, mood, lifestyle, body, beliefs, jobs, friends. The list is virtually endless. No matter how good or bad you may think your life is, it can change for the better. No matter how young or how old you are, you can be healthier and happier.

Not long ago, aging was a dirty word. People were considered old, over the hill, ready to be put out to pasture after retirement, sometimes sooner. Old age came with labels like isolation, frustration, disability, inactivity, dowdy and cranky. No more! Today the word old doesn't fit the majority of seniors. They're leading active, dynamic lives — socializing, exercising, learning, traveling, and falling in love again. They're proof that…

Aging has changed.
It's time to change our mind about aging.

From the moment we're born, we're aging. At each stage of development, we have different goals and face different challenges. While this book is aimed primarily at people entering and living in the latter half of their lives, it has valuable information for people at every age and stage of life.

MAKE THE BEST OF THE REST OF YOUR LIFE evolved from lectures I present on cruise ships. My audiences come from all over the world and have widely diversified backgrounds, but when they walk into the theater to hear my presentations, I know they have several things in common. They want to better themselves, sharpen their minds, improve their lives. No matter how educated and accomplished they are, they are willing to learn and grow.

You fall into this category or you wouldn't be reading this book. In a sense, you are boarding a ship with me, about to take a voyage. Today is embarkation day. Your present age is your port of departure. Where are we going? We're sailing toward a bright, exciting future.

Along the way, you'll see negative misperceptions about aging crumble and fall, discover how aging has changed, and read the latest information regarding physical, mental and emotional health. You'll learn how your mind and memory work, and how you can make better use of your amazing brain. You'll also find out what constitutes happiness, and how attitude and laughter affect well-being. By using the information in this book, you will be able to take command of your personal ship of life and make the best of your voyage.

Who am I to be leading you on this journey? I've been teaching, lecturing and writing about self-development and the power of mind since the early 1980s. My first book was a forerunner of the self-help movement. In 2002 I began lecturing on cruise ships all over the world on these subjects. It is due to the urging and encouragement of my audiences that I wrote this book.

My interest in aging goes back to the late 1970s when I worked for a time as the activity director of a nursing home. It became a subject of special concern toward the end of 2000 when my mother suddenly lost her short-term memory. Thanks to my husband's knowledge of health and our combined research, we found many supplements that I credit to some degree with significantly slowing the progression of her dementia. But mostly, I credit her attitude. My mother eventually had to enter a nursing home due to her poor memory and some other problems, but she remained alert and witty and wise in the moment.

Always a strong, self-sufficient woman, I watched her go through difficult transitions — from an independent life to residing with my brother and his wonderful family, then into an assisted living facility and finally a nursing home. Each relocation was accompanied by some depression. Time and again, I saw my mother remind herself that she had a choice, and pull herself out of it.

What bothered her most was the belief that she was a burden to others. In fact, she was a ray of sunshine to everyone who knew her. When I told her the title of this book, she said, "I'm not a very good example." But she's the best example I know because she truly made the best of a most difficult situation. Even though she lost her independence and had to rely on others for things most of us take for granted, she continued to smile and laugh and give unlimited love to family, friends and the wonderful people who cared for her. One nurse told me that she looked forward to coming to work just to see Nancy.

My mother had what I consider the most essential qualities for happiness at any age: a positive attitude and a loving nature. She always urged me to make the most of myself and the best of whatever happens. More than ever, she practiced what she preached in the final stages of her life. As I watched her make the best of ever diminishing circumstances, I also learned a great deal about courage.

> *Courage is the power to let go of the familiar.*
> — *Raymond Lindquist*

A man was enjoying a leisurely hike through the forest one day. All of a sudden, he heard a rustling sound. He turned and saw a mountain lion less than thirty feet away. The animal cast hungry eyes upon the hiker and made a threatening growl. The hiker took off at top speed running deeper and deeper into the woods, fear building with every step.

Finally he spotted an opening in the trees and ran toward it. He jumped across the tree line and to his horror discovered he had jumped off a cliff. As he fell, he caught hold of a small tree growing from the side of the mountain. Under his weight, the limbs began to crack.

The hiker looked up and saw the lion licking his chops. He looked down at the bottomless abyss. He knew it was only moments before he'd plummet to his death. There was no place to go, nothing left to do but pray.

He raised his eyes to the sky and cried, "God, if you're up there, help me. I know I haven't been much of a believer but I need you now. If you exist, if you're up there, I'm begging you, tell me what to do."

There was a crack of thunder and then God's Voice bellowed from the heavens: "Let go, my child."

The man looked down at the abyss, up at the hungry mountain lion, raised his eyes to the skies once more and yelled, "Is anybody else up there?"

We are all hikers through the forest of life. Just when we think we know the territory and feel safe, something appears to push us over the edge, past our comfort zone. The tendency is to grab onto the old and familiar, and hold on for dear life. But our safety nets have become frayed and can no longer support us. We feel ourselves falling off the cliff, and fear there is no place to go except down. But there is another alternative.

"Come to the cliff," the Papa Bird said to his babies.

"No, no," they cried.

"Come to the cliff," he said.

"We are afraid," they cried.

"Come to the cliff," he commanded.

They came. He pushed them. They flew.

Years ago, a friend asked me to address her third grade class and tell them about the power of thought. As I told them they could do anything they set their minds to, one little boy became increasingly excited. Finally he jumped out of his seat and yelled, "But can I fly? Can I fly?" That was probably the hardest question I ever had to answer; the last thing I wanted to do was dampen his enthusiasm.

"Yes," I finally said. "You can fly. Not all by yourself perhaps, but in an airplane or with a parachute or a kite. And you can even fly all by yourself in your dreams. But more important, you can fly with your dreams. And they will take you wherever you want to go."

Every stage of life requires jumping off a cliff. Whether we fall or fly depends on our willingness to let go of the familiar and enter the unknown. Nature's Law of the Vacuum applies to the mind as well: opposite things cannot occupy the same space at the same time. Love and hate cannot co-exist, happiness and sadness, trust and fear, hope and despair, holding on and letting go. We can't cling to the past, base our identity on former achievements, be bound by the familiar, and be fully alive — learning and growing — in the present.

Life is a process of becoming,
a combination of states we have to go through.
Where people fail is that they wish to elect a state
and remain in it. This is a kind of death.
— Anais Nin

Life is growth, and growth requires change. We are changing every day, every hour, every second. Every thought that passes through your mind changes the configuration of your brain, and affects your emotional and physical state. Resistance to change is resistance to life, and...

RESISTANCE CAUSES PAIN!

There came a time when the risk to remain tight in the bud
was more painful than the risk it took to blossom.
— Anais Nin

Resisting the natural changes and stages of life is like trying to hold back a raging river. Guess who wins. You'll drown unless you turn around and go with the flow. As you will see in the pages ahead, a thought, a laugh, a smile, a walk can turn you around, and start your energy moving in the right direction. But you have to be willing to let go of the old and embrace the great unknown that lies ahead.

Courage does not mean that we jump off the cliff without fear.

It means we jump in spite of it.

Life will push us forward, whether we like it or not. Whatever our mountain lion may be, whatever pushes us over the edge of the cliff, we should be grateful for. If it were not for that push, we might never let go, and if we don't let go, we won't grow.

So, say goodbye to the past, the old safety nets, the myths and misperceptions about aging. Prepare for an exciting adventure as we sail into uncharted territory. Never before in history have people lived so long. Join the millions who are blazing trails into a new stage of human development and making the best of the rest of their life.

SUGGESTED READING:
Second Passages by Gail Sheehy

QUOTES TO LIVE BY:

> *All changes, even the most longed for, have their melancholy.*
> *For what we leave behind us is a part of ourselves;*
> *we must die to one life before we can enter another.*
> — *Anatole France*

Chapter 2

BREAKING THE MOLD

Do not follow where the path may lead. Go, instead, where there is no path and leave a trail.

Ralph Waldo Emerson

A 60 year old man went to the doctor for a complete physical check up. When he returned several days later for the results, the doctor told him, "You're in terrific shape! You have the body of a 30 year old. At the rate you're going, you're going to live a long, long time. How old was your father when he died?"

"Did I say he was dead?" replied the patient.

"Your father is still alive?" said the doctor. "That's wonderful. How old is he and what kind of shape is he in?"

The man responded, "My father is 82 years old and he's in great shape. He snow skis in winter and water skis in summer."

"That's terrific," said the doctor. "Good for him. Well, what about your grandfather? How old was he when he died?"

"Did I say he was dead?"

The doctor was astonished. "You mean to tell me you are 60 years old and both your father and grandfather are still alive? That's amazing. Well, tell me, how old is your grandfather and what kind of shape is he in?"

"My grandfather is 103 and he's in terrific shape. He walks two miles a day and swims three times a week. Not only that, he's getting married next week!"

"Wow!" said the doctor. "Good for him. But I have to ask you, why would a 103 year old man want to get married?"

"Did I say he wanted to?"

Aging has changed. It's time to change our mind about aging!

It's time to stop making false assumptions about the senior years and lay to rest a lot of old beliefs. First, the facts...

The average American life expectancy is presently 77.9 years. According to census statistics, there are 41 countries in the world with longer life expectancies. Number one at 83.5 years is the little country of Andorra between Spain and France. Japan is second at almost 82 years, and more people live past 100 in Okinawa than anywhere else. (Note: The people of Hunza, Pakistan were not included in the study.) Australia, New Zealand, the countries of Western Europe, Israel and Singapore also have longer life expectancies than the United States.

Among the reasons the United States lags behind:
  A steep rise in obesity, diabetes and depression
  Increased consumption of sugary, caffeinated beverages instead of water
  Decline in the consumption of natural foods
  Diet high in fats, sugars and processed foods

High levels of stress

Lack of exercise

We're living longer than ever before, but if we want to enjoy those extra years, we must take care of ourselves and nurture the qualities that make for a long, healthy, happy life. What are they? Various research studies come up with the same conclusion: LIFESTYLE, LIFESTYLE, LIFESTYLE.

We are responsible for how we age.

After the mid-50s, 70% of aging is controlled by lifestyle. Genes tilt us in certain directions, but whether or not we follow depends to a large degree on choices we make. A person may have a genetic disposition toward heart disease, for instance, but lifestyle and environment play a significant role in whether s/he actually develops it. Things can be done to cut the risk of heart disease, frailty, Alzheimer's, and many other illnesses and disabilities. We can begin at any time to increase our health and well-being, live longer and live better. The sooner we start, the greater the rewards. But the rewards are great no matter when we start.

This book is all about developing a lifestyle that gives us the body, mind and attitude we need to live a long, healthy, happy life. Nothing special is needed. You can start right now, right where you are. You'll begin to turn the tide almost immediately. For instance…

If you quit smoking, circulation immediately improves and the lungs start repairing damage. After one smoke-free year, risk of heart disease, stroke, lung disease and cancer falls.

If you're overweight, losing 5 - 10% of your body weight and eating a nutritional diet low in fats and sugars can lower blood pressure, help prevent type 2 diabetes and slow the aging process.

You can build your brain by growing dendrites at any age. Ongoing mental stimulation and learning lessen the risk of dementia.

Alzheimer's Disease is the most common form of dementia and developing it is the number one fear of aging people. The good news: Dementia is not an inevitable aspect of aging. In Okinawa, Japan, seniors have one-third less dementia than Americans. They also experience one-fifth of the heart disease, and one-fourth of the breast and prostate cancer of Americans. I guess that's why so many live past 100.

There are things we can do to reverse negative trends and greatly improve our quality of life. Exercise has a major impact on physical, psychological and emotional well-being. With ongoing learning, we can build better brains. With desire and commitment, we can live healthy, happy, fulfilling lives.

If one advances confidently in the direction of his dreams
and endeavors to live the life which he has imagined,
he will meet with a success unexpected in common hours.
— Henry David Thoreau

Today, seniors are advancing in the direction of their dreams like never before. Not too long ago, empty nest syndrome and retirement were hallmarks of declining years. Today, they signal new beginnings. The beginning of new lifestyles, new pursuits, new experiences. We are now living long enough to have three or four or more entirely different life stories in one life span. And many aren't waiting until retirement to do so. They are changing course mid-stream, relocating, starting second and third careers, developing new interests.

Many retirees work part or full time. Older workers consistently rank higher than younger colleagues in dependability, loyalty, good judgment and responsibility. They take fewer sick days and have less accidents. A 103 year old Japanese woman worked as a seamstress until she was 99. Retired people are going into local politics, traveling extensively, writing books, painting, resuming their education, joining local theater groups, taking college courses, and doing volunteer work. Many are living and traveling in motor homes. Others are seeing the world on cruise ships and freighters. For those who like to travel and volunteer, there are many organizations offering that opportunity. Google 'overseas volunteers.'

The opportunities for creative aging are truly endless. Grandma Moses took up painting when she was 75 and created 1,600 canvases by the time she died at 101. "If I didn't start painting," she said, "I would have raised chickens."

After 12 years as a widower, a man in Italy, tired of being alone and lonely, put an ad in newspapers around the country announcing that he was available for adoption as a grandparent. From the many replies he received, he chose a family of four. They moved him into their large home and were soon calling him Grandpa. "I've turned a new page," he says happily. "I recommend other lonely people get adopted."

One of the most common regrets of seniors is that they didn't complete or further their education. Why not now? Seniors are returning to college in record numbers whether it be to audit a class or for credit. Some colleges offer senior summer school programs. In one of my lectures, an 85 year old proudly told me that she entered graduate school at the age of 73 to pursue a Master's Degree. She went on to earn her Ph.D. at the age of 81. Of her experience, Florence says, "I was able to share intimate knowledge of unique events of the 20th century in which I had been a participant. Courageous aging recaptures the life potential of the older adult and challenges the younger person toward multi-cultural and intergenerational partnerships."

Nearly one half of the 65 — 74 population does some type of volunteer work. In schools, their knowledge and skills are providing students with much needed one on one time and tutoring. They are acting as surrogate grandparents and mentors.

> *Had it not been for the love, intelligence and courage*
> *of that woman (her mentor), I would just be another*
> *black girl raped in the dirt roads of Arkansas.*
> — *Maya Angelou*

Nowhere is there more evidence of the new senior lifestyle than in sports. In recent years:

An 88 year old woman won the women's 85 and over tennis championship.

An 82 year old holds the men's senior world record for the 100 yard dash.

A 78 year old rode his bike from Canada to Mexico in 10 days, 15 hours.

A 70 year old became the oldest person to swim the English Channel.

In 2003, a 99 year old Japanese man skied Mont Blanc's Vallee Blanche. His 70 year old son is the oldest person to climb Mt. Everest.

Think such people are in perfect health to start with? Not too many years ago, a polio and cancer survivor won the slalom and tricks event at the National Water Ski Championships. She racked up an impressive score even though there were no other competitors in her age group. She was 91.

Seniors are growing in number and their numbers are growing in power. So, let's set the record straight…

SENIORS...

Have financial clout. People over 50 control more than 70 % of the wealth in the United States.

Know what's going on. Almost 70% of adults over 65 read newspapers on a daily basis, the highest percentage of any age group.

Are good citizens. Seniors generally have a larger voter turnout than other age groups.

For the most part are active and happy with retirement.

One research study concluded: "There is increasing momentum toward the emergence of a physically and cognitively fit, non-disabled, active elderly population."

Aging has changed. It's time to change our mind about aging!

The old stereotypes don't fit anymore. It's time to perceive the senior years as the exciting, fulfilling time of life they can be. Have you always wanted to pursue photography, acting, writing, painting, travel, boating, dancing, archeology, environmental causes? Whatever you have dreamed of doing, learning, exploring, now is the time to start because...

Now is the time to make the best of the rest of your life!

SUGGESTED READING:

The Power of Experience Edited by Jeremy James

MORE INFORMATION:

AARP Magazine and AARP Newsletter

www.aarp.org; www.seniorjournal.com

QUOTES TO LIVE BY:

> *To me old age is always fifteen years older than I am.*
> *– Bernard Baruch on his 85th birthday*

Chapter 3

HAPPINESS: THE REAL THING

I think everybody should get rich and famous and do everything they ever dreamed of so they can see that it's not the answer.

Jim Carrey

Everyone at every age wants to be happy. Sadly, many people are going in the opposite direction. Depression in the United States is ten times greater than it was in the 1960s. The median age then for the onset of the first bout of depression was 29.5. Today, it's 14.5. The statistics are similar in many developed countries. China and India, the two fastest growing economies in the world, are also experiencing psychological repercussions resulting from job demands, high stress, materialism and the overall Westernization of their cultures.

In 2006, researchers at Britain's University of Leicester published results from a study of happiness levels in 178 countries. The United Kingdom came in 41st, Australia 26th and the United States 23rd. Smaller countries with more social cohesion and national identity tended to score better. Aidrian White, analytic social psychologist, said population size plays a role in a nation's level of happiness.

That proved true in the 2005 World Values Survey. Venezuela, Nigeria and the Philippines ranked higher than Australia, the USA, and the United Kingdom in the number of people who consider themselves 'very happy.' Although poverty levels are elevated in these countries, they share a high value for and celebration of family and community.

In the United States, people are working harder and longer, have more possessions and prosperity than ever before but are no happier than people were in the 1950s. In fact, divorce, abuse, crime, and suicide rates have escalated significantly. The World Value Survey happiness researchers are among those who believe that consumerism is actually a deterrent to real happiness. Therapist Sherry Cardinal says, "A number one stressor for Americans is consumer related pressure. Striving after bigger, newer and better while going deeper and longer in debt keeps us fearful and awake nights."

Psychologist Abraham Maslow developed a hierarchy of human needs in the 1940s. It is generally demonstrated as a pyramid with five levels that define the human experience. The first two levels are concerned strictly with survival. Until those needs are met, people don't have the time, energy or motivation to strive for anything beyond them.

Level 1: Physiological/biological needs: Breathing, food, water, sleep.

Level 2: Security: Shelter, stability, safety.

Level 3: Relationships: The need to belong. Relationships with family, friends, community.

Level 4: Esteem: Achievement, recognition, respect.

Level 5: Self actualization: Fulfilling potential, higher meaning and purpose, transcendent experience.

According to Maslow, the higher we move, the more we realize true happiness. In consumer driven societies, many people are stuck on Level 2 seeking fulfillment in more possessions, better shelters, greater stability. They're not finding it. One study published in a magazine several years ago determined that a South African farmer earning $200 a year is about as happy as an American worker earning $70,000 a year. **After basic needs are met, money does not affect level of happiness**. In fact, the law of diminishing returns goes into effect: Additional acquisitions bring less and less happiness.

In a national Australian survey in 2002, Clive Hamilton of the Australia Institute found that a higher percentage of low income earners (under $25,000 a year) were happy and more satisfied with life than high income earners. "Instead of wondering whether the desire for more money is the problem," he said, "they (people) raise their threshold of desire; this is an endless cycle."

The Hunza people in Pakistan live about two miles up in the Himalayas and 60 miles from a modern settlement. They have no jails, hospitals, banks, prisoners, sickness or money. Living and working past 100 is common. One observer claimed that one reason they live long, healthy, happy lives is, "Hunzakats have enough of everything, but just about."

It's wonderful to move from nothing to having enough. But once there, having more brings less and less satisfaction. In spite of extensive research supporting these conclusions, the drive for money is on the rise. Between 1970 and 1990, the percentage of college students who ranked financial success above all other goals doubled. It rose to 74% while those who most valued a meaningful life dropped from 76% to 43%.

While prosperity and consumerism were on the rise, happiness was not. More people than ever sought psychological counseling but the majority failed to improve based solely on the therapy. As the success of traditional psychotherapy was being questioned, a new Science of Positive Psychology was being born. It focuses on positive emotions instead of negative ones, emphasizes building on one's strengths instead of dwelling on weaknesses. The first class was offered at Harvard in 2003. Six students signed up. By 2006, it was being taught across the nation and was the most popular class at Harvard with a registration of 855 students.

At every age and stage of life, we all seek happiness. If it could easily be attained, we'd all have it. Perhaps one reason it eludes us is that we are not certain what happiness really is, and search for it in the wrong places. Happiness is often confused with pleasure.

HAPPINESS = consistent, contented state of mind, inner peace, general sense of well-being.

PLEASURE = transitory sensory experiences: food, excitement, temporary gratification.

Happiness comes from inside out.
Pleasure comes from outside in.

Martin Seligman, one of the founders of Positive Psychology and author of Authentic Happiness says, "When we engage in pleasures, we are perhaps just consuming." Craving pleasure is actually a sign of unhappiness.

Unhappiness is the effect of low self-esteem, self-absorption, lack of meaning, setting grandiose, unrealistic goals. If we had to put it in one word, that word would be NEGATIVITY! Negativity = self-defeating thoughts, pessimistic expectations, critical attitude, seeing self as victim, thinking in absolute terms: Nothing ever works out for me; people always take advantage of me.

MRIs (Magnetic Resonance Imaging) have shown that happy/hopeful thoughts have a calming effect on the brain while negative ones inflame areas of the brain involved with depression and anxiety. Happiness is essential to psychological and physical well-being. Compared to unhappy people, happy people have younger hearts and arteries, stronger immune systems, lower blood pressure and recover faster from surgery.

> *Happiness is not a destination. It is a method of life.*
> — *Burton Hillis*

Don't despair if you are not as happy as you'd like to be. Unhappy people can become happy, and happy people can become happier. By focusing our efforts on the things that create happiness, we will naturally develop a more satisfying, fulfilling life.

HAPPINESS...

Is a state of being not having.
Does not come from the world but from yourself.
Is based on attitude not achievement.
Depends on how you react to what happens not what happens.

SUGGESTED READING: *Authentic Happiness: Using the New Positive Psychology to Realize Your Potential for Lasting Fulfillment* by Martin Seligman

MORE INFORMATION: www.h2u.com; www.authentichappiness.com

QUOTES TO LIVE BY:

> *The Constitution only guarantees the American people the right to pursue happiness. You have to catch it yourself.*
> – *Benjamin Franklin*

Chapter 4

HAPPINESS: THE FOUNDATION

Happiness is not a goal;
it is a by-product.
Eleanir Roosevlt

A 6 year old told her mother that she wanted a magic wand for her birthday. "And this time," she said, "I want one that works." Don't we eall? Don't we wish we could wave a magic wand and be happy? But happiness is a journey, a process, a talent that must be developed and nurtured.

The following qualities compose the foundation of happiness. They are not listed in any particular order. They're intertwined, activating and reinforcing each other. As we develop and nurture these aspects of our lives, we experience happiness.

1. SELF-ESTEEM

A man cannot be comfortable without his own approval.
—Mark Twain

Self-esteem by definition must come from within one's self. It is confidence in your own worth as an individual. Character is at the root of self-esteem. How you perceive and feel about yourself day to day, hour to hour is the strongest indicator of your level of happiness. If you don't respect yourself, like and value your own being, there will be a void inside that nothing external can fill up.

Who are you? Would you be friends with you? Do business with you? Go to you for advice? How do your friends describe you? How do you imagine strangers see you? Are people comfortable around you? What do you value most in yourself? Do you feel competent? Describe the person you would like to be. How are you like that person? How are you different? What would you change about yourself?

There's no denying that appearance is important in our world. It accounts for 55% of a first impression. How we look and dress also affects how we feel about ourselves. People with high self-esteem take good care of themselves BUT taking care of yourself raises self-esteem.

2. THOUGHTS

> *The happiness of your life depends on the quality of your thoughts.*
> *– Marcus A. Antoninus*

Change your mind and you change your life. I read an inspiring story about a 92-year-old man who had to move into a nursing home when his wife died. After filling out the paper work, he was led to his room by a social worker. She described it on the way.

"Oh, I love it!" he interrupted with enthusiasm.

Taken aback, she replied, "But you haven't seen it yet."

"That doesn't have anything to do with it," he said. **"Happiness is something you decide on ahead of time.** Whether I like my room or not doesn't depend on how the furniture is arranged... it's how I arrange my mind. I already decided to love it."

Happiness is something we decide on ahead of time! It's an intention, a commitment. Happiness and unhappiness are both mindsets, lens through which we view the world. What we see outside is a reflection of what's going on inside. **The world is our mirror. What does your world look like?**

Years ago, I was addressing the nursing staff of a hospital. At the end of my talk, one nurse asked how to handle a particularly difficult patient. When she mentioned the room number, a colleague cried, "Oh, you can't mean Mr. X! He's the sweetest person on the floor."

People can meet the same person, look at the same object, hear the same words, and have entirely different interpretations and reactions. It all depends on individual perception. Your unique experience, conditioning, prejudices, values all color what you see and influence your perception. But perception can be changed.

> A 5 year old boy came home from kindergarten and excitedly told his mother what he had learned about the Red Cross Bloodmobile that day.

> "It would be a terrible thing if the Bloodmobile ever got in an accident," he concluded. Then suddenly he cried, "No, wait! That would be a good thing because if anyone needed the blood, it would be right there."

It's all in the way we look and there's always another way to look at things. That is one of the greatest powers a human being has. We can change our minds. If you don't like what you're seeing, change the lens you're looking through and look again. Here is one of the simplest and most powerful laws of mind:

Your brain seeks and finds what you're looking for.

What are you looking for? Everything you experience is affected by your perception. It all starts with thought including...

3. ACTIONS

Life consists in penetrating the unknown, and fashioning our actions
in accord with the new knowledge thus acquired.

— *Leo Tolstoy*

Happiness may be your goal but attaining it requires action. We create through action. Action is the bridge over which invisible thoughts and feelings pass into the visible world. Actions reflect who and what we are, how we feel about ourselves and others. They can make or break self-esteem, relationships, health.

Immobility depletes energy, leads to boredom and depression. We learn and grow and achieve through action. We connect to others through action. Happiness is expressed through action. Volunteering is a highly rewarding activity to many people because it incorporates several of the threads of happiness: social interaction, giving, purpose and kindness — the most nourishing act of all.

Three things in human life are important.
The first is to be kind. The second is to be kind. The third is to be kind.

— *Henry James*

Kindness can't be over-rated. It activates good feelings in giver and receiver; feelings that last long after the act is over. In one experiment, college students were divided into two groups. One was told to perform some act of kindness that evening and the other was to indulge in a pleasurable activity. By the time the class met the next day, the thrill of pleasurable pursuits was long over. Students who had performed an act of kindness, however, were still basking in the warm feelings generated. Many later reported that their whole day went better.

4. GOOD RELATIONSHIPS

Age does not protect you from love
but love to some extent protects you from age.
— *Jeanne Moreau*

The quality of one's relationships is directly related to levels of self-esteem and happiness. Caring relatives and friends make good times better and bad times more bearable. People with good, close, supportive relationships are happier, experience less illness and live longer than those without. It isn't only receiving support that makes us happy, it's giving support to others. Being compassionate and emotionally generous significantly raises our worth — in our own eyes as well as others'.

The support of family and friends, particularly a spouse, decreases the risk of developing dementia and cardiovascular disease. A good marriage is one of the strongest factors in happy aging. A harmonious relationship and affectionate physical contact have positive biological effects. Conversely, the stress of conflict with a partner can reduce the antibodies in the blood, lowering immune defenses against disease.

Social engagement lessens the likelihood of cognitive impairment while social isolation has a negative impact on health, attitude and behavior. Loneliness is often at the root of alcohol abuse, stress and depression which in turn increase the likelihood of developing heart disease. A sudden personality change such as an outgoing personality becoming withdrawn can be a sign of depression or the onset of dementia.

One of the dangers of aging is shrinking social circles. Fortunately we're never too old to make new friends. Longtime relationships provide security, but new ones are stimulating and expand our boundaries. One of the great benefits of traveling is meeting interesting people and making new friends. Being active in church, community and volunteer programs are also excellent ways to develop and maintain a strong social circle.

5. FAITH

Life without faith in something is too narrow a space to live.
— *George Lancaster Spalding*

Mother Theresa said that the spiritual suffering she observed in the prosperous West rivaled the physical suffering she saw in the slums of Calcutta. That's a strong statement but it is supported by various studies that found people with faith suffer less depression and are better able to cope with stressful situations. They live longer, experience less pain, recover from surgery faster, and are three times more likely to survive open-heart surgery.

Having faith does not necessarily involve religious belief or practice. Simply trusting in a power greater than one's self aids us in achieving a more positive, hopeful outlook, greater health and happiness. Faith gives people strength, courage and peace of mind as well as endowing life with purpose and meaning.

6. PURPOSE

If you don't know where you are going,
you will probably end up somewhere else.
— *Lawrence J. Peter*

Everyone has a purpose in life. Whether it's survival or spiritual enlightenment or any of the infinite possibilities in between, your life is motivated by purpose. **Consciously or unconsciously, there is a purpose to everything we do.** One of the primary qualities of happy people at all ages is having a positive purpose.

What is your purpose? What makes you happy? What gives you a sense of fulfillment? Successful aging requires that there be a meaningful purpose to one's life. It is your responsibility to define it and pursue it.

When we are working or raising a family, our purpose seems clear and unquestionable. What happens when the children are grown, out on their own, and career ends in retirement? Even if you looked forward to it, retirement is a major transition. You are stepping into a new world and must re-define your identity.

At such a time, it is not uncommon a to feel purposeless. If that feeling is prolonged, self-esteem starts to plummet. The longer we go without purpose, the more we rely on the past for identity and self-worth, and the greater the risk of unhappiness, depression and withdrawal. While change and growth often arouse fear and resistance, we have the power to rise above those feelings and forge ahead.

People who find a new purpose and re-create themselves are the ones who find happiness in retirement. Purpose provides identity, drive and enthusiasm. Whether you find inspiration in a hobby, improving your health and relationships or helping others, you will feel that you have a raison d'etre, a reason for being.

Sometimes life hands us a completely unexpected purpose, as in the case of Barbara and Dan of Calgary, Canada. We met them in an RV park in Jasper, Canada during the summer of 2001. When they maneuvered their trailer into the spot next to us, I saw four adorable children emerge. How nice, I thought, for grandparents to be taking their grandchildren on a camping trip. But Barbara and Dan were more than grandparents.

BARBARA'S STORY

Dan and I are 76 and 67 years of age and have been raising a second family of four children for the past 5 years. Dan's dream of retirement was to travel. He does travel now but it is as a parent supervisor for school field trips, transporting the children to birthday parties, to and from swim lessons, hockey games, and basketball or soccer practices. My greatest expectation was freedom. Freedom to go anywhere we wished without ever again having to juggle work schedules and time tables. Also I wanted freedom to pursue my interests in quilting and interior decorating. Instead of gaining freedom, I stepped back 30 years and became a fulltime mother again.

Our children, three boys and one girl, are Bradly 10, Mark 8, Darien 6 and Cameron 5. They are the children of our youngest daughter who we adopted. Her parents were both alcoholics and she was born with alcohol related disabilities. When she married, she chose someone with the same background and problems she had, and the cycle of drugs, alcohol, neglect and physical abuse continued.

Dan and I tried to help them during the first few years but soon realized we were only enabling them to continue the lifestyle they had chosen. It was heart wrenching to imagine how the withdrawal of our support might affect the children. Thankfully, each month when their money was gone they brought the children to stay with us until the next payday. The day came when the violence was extreme enough to involve the police. The call that came in the middle of that night changed the course of our lives.

When the children came to live with us, they had numerous physical, emotional, and learning problems. I immediately began arranging for speech therapy, medical needs which had been neglected, kindergarten registration for Bradly, and early intervention for Mark and Darien. These sound like routine things and they are if you are a parent. But as a grandparent you encounter roadblocks at every turn. Without the parent's consent you cannot do the simplest things for the children. I spent hours on the phone every day and shed many tears of frustration trying to find help and information. Not wanting the involvement of social services in our lives, I obtained all of the necessary papers from the courts and filed for private guardianship. We were successful and this was a tremendous help.

The arrival of the children brought many changes to our life. At times it was overwhelming to think that these changes would be permanent. Our interests now revolved around the children's school activities. Vacation choices were made with the children in mind. One of the saddest changes in our life has been the loss of friends. Our interests and priorities are no longer the same as theirs. As time passed we had less in common and drifted apart.

I miss being a grandmother. Although these children are my grandchildren, I am also their mother. However, our lives have a new and important purpose. Raising a second family has been a wonderful experience. It has kept us in touch with the simpler things in life and kept us thinking young. It is an opportunity to once again see things through the eyes of a child, and it is a joy to see the children learn.

No problems are insurmountable when you approach them one day at a time. Prayer and dependence on God give us daily strength. Sometimes we felt our age was a disadvantage, but our maturity and experience have given us the ability to determine the special needs of the children and knowledge of the avenues to take to find intervention for them. We know we are making a positive difference.

It gives us a sense of peace and satisfaction to know that we have been able to give the children a start in life that otherwise they would never have had. We have also been able to provide them with a sense of family. The children bring love and laughter to our lives. Their hugs and "I love you's" are our reward.

We all make plans for our life after retirement. It may be to travel, take university courses, do volunteer work, or any number of things. But for some of us these plans will never become a reality. That should not deter us from having a wonderful retirement. Although Dan and I still make long-term plans, we try to spend more time appreciating today, enjoying the simpler things in life. I would urge people not to get caught up in all the have-to-do's, to include small things which bring peace and contentment. Our retirement years may not be what we had envisioned but they have brought new joys we had not anticipated.

Self-esteem, a positive outlook, kindness, good relationships, faith and purpose — these form the foundation of happiness. If you are not as happy as you would like to be, there's great news. Recent research has concluded that happiness can be lastingly increased.

SUGGESTED READING:
The Art of Happiness: A Handbook for Living
by HH Dalai Lama and Howard C. Cutler

QUOTES TO LIVE BY:

> *Happiness is when what you think, what you say,*
> *and what you do are in harmony.*
> — *Mahatma Gandhi*

Chapter 5

BUILDING BLOCKS

There are only two ways to live your life:

One is as though nothing is a miracle. The other is as if everything is.

I believe in the latter.

Albert Einstein

If you have the foundation for happiness, you can weather any storm. Losses and setbacks may shake you, but your foundation will provide strength and support. Some schools of thought claim that we have a 'set point' for happiness, a baseline level which is influenced by our genes. If that is true, it's no more than 50%, and research on the brain has demonstrated that it can be changed. We can build on the foundation and raise our 'set point.'

But are you willing to do so? Are you willing to accept that your life, your happiness and how you feel at any time are your...

1. RESPONSIBILITY

A man sooner or later discovers that
he is the master-gardener of his soul, the director of his life.
— James Allen

I like to think of responsibility as RESPONSE-ABILITY. We may not have control over what happens to us but we always have a choice in how we respond to what happens. In the play, *A Death in the Family*, James Agee penned these words: "It's a kind of a test, Mary, and it's the only kind that amounts to anything. When something rotten like this happens, then you have your choice. You start to really be alive, or you start to die. That's all."

You have your choice. Learn, grow, forgive, be a bigger, better person — start to really be alive. Or start to die because when we stop learning and growing, we begin to wither. It's a matter of choice. How we interpret an incident or view a person, the meaning we assign to something, all choices. Perception, reaction, attitude, all choices. These choices not only determine how we feel, they influence what we experience.

The brain and the eye may have a contractual relationship in which the brain has agreed to believe what the eye sees, but in return the eye has agreed to look for what the brain wants.

— *Daniel Gilbert*

It's a cycle of cause and effect. An experience may cause me to develop a certain perception. But that perception then causes me to have more of those experiences because that's what I'm looking for. My brain looks for what I expect. **What do you expect? What do you want? What are you looking for?**

My father was a minister and the sermon I best recall was given one New Year's Day. He proposed that every year should be the best year of our life because we bring to it all the experience and learning and love and laughter of the years that have gone before. Obviously, we have setbacks along the way. There may be health or money problems. We may lose loved ones. But ideally, the richness of the life we have lived has stored memories and skills and attitudes in our internal bank that give us the strength to rise up, mentally if not physically, and make the best of each new year.

Hopefully, we come to the latter years with a clear knowledge of who we are, a positive purpose and strong personal relationships. If we haven't, now is the time to do so because no one else is going to do it for us. If you expect life or other people to be responsible for your happiness, you have assumed the mindset of a victim and forfeited personal power. Victims may enjoy blaming others but they don't enjoy life. They do not feel in control of their happiness and well-being, and feeling some degree of control over one's life is essential to self-confidence and happiness.

> *The best years of your life are the ones in which you decide*
> *your problems are your own. You do not blame them on*
> *your mother, the ecology, or the president.*
> *You realize that you control your own destiny.*
> — *Albert Ellis*

Though we may rely on others for help and guidance, we are responsible for our own well-being. After his doctor put him on one of the cholesterol lowering drugs, one senior told me that he went home and studied the drug for himself. He went back to the doctor with the knowledge he acquired. The doctor listened, read some of the material his patient gave him, and immediately lowered the dose. That man is now doing just as well without the risk of as many side effects.

In early 2008, the results of several clinical trials raised questions about the effects of cholesterol lowering drugs. If you're taking a statin, it would behoove you to check the latest research. No one should take any drug without personally studying the side-effects and contraindications. Do not rely on your doctor to tell you. *The Physician's Desk Reference* and *The Pill Book* are two of several books available for sale to the general public that provide information about drugs. Also check the interactions between various medications you may be taking. There is a wealth of health and drug information on the internet on sites like www.peoplespharmacy.com.

2. FORGIVENESS

The weak can never forgive.
Forgiveness is the attribute of the strong.
— *Mahatma Gandhi*

It's been said that resentment is like drinking poison and hoping the other person will die. That's not just a metaphor. Hate is literally poison to the body and brain. Whether it is ourselves or someone else we refuse to forgive, we damage ourselves on every level. Prolonged feelings of hate and resentment increase blood pressure and heart rate, depress the immune system, cause headaches and deplete energy. Carrying grievances erodes peace and happiness, and leads to depression. The anger, grief and resentment inherent in one unforgiving thought leeches out to all areas of the mind and colors perception.

Bad things do happen to good people and grieving is a necessary part of the healing process. But so is forgiveness. Dwelling on negative experiences and memories injects them with power. One of the laws of life is the Law of Praise: What you praise with your thoughts, words and feelings increases. In other words, praise is like fertilizer. It makes things grow. Focusing on bad experiences increases pain and resentment. Learn the lesson and move on. Forgiveness has positive physical, mental and emotional effects. It releases tension, raises self-esteem and strengthens relationships. So take your power and peace back. Be quick to forgive.

3. COPE-ABILITY

If you break your neck, if you have nothing to eat,
if your house is on fire, then you got a problem.
Everything else is inconvenience.
— *Robert Fulghum*

Living in Florida, we've witnessed some nasty hurricanes. After they pass and people go out to view the damage, it always amazes me that the graceful and flexible palms are still standing while huge trees with big heavy trunks lie on the ground, pulled up by their roots. The trees that survive the storms are those that bend with the wind. People who best weather storms share that flexibility.

Successful aging requires a strong but adaptable nature. A study of 500 adults ages 60 - 98 found optimism and coping skills were more important than health to aging happily. One of the characteristics that people who live past 100 share is a sense of control over their lives. Another is adaptability. The two are not incompatible. In addition to being self-directed and making plans, we need to adapt when life doesn't go as expected. Flexible people accept life's curve balls and maintain inner peace even when things go awry. They are more relaxed, easier to be around, and adjust to situations rather than trying to force situations to adjust to them.

One reason many people have difficulty coping with retirement is that they haven't planned for it. Have you made plans for life after work? Do you know where you're going to live, how you're going to spend your time and how you're going to pay for it? A major cause of stress is not being financially prepared for the latter years of life. It is never too soon to start planning for retirement income and making arrangements for long-term care should that become necessary. And don't think long-term care is just for seniors. 32%

of the people who suffer a stroke and 40% of those receiving long-term care are under 65!

> *The past is behind, learn from it.*
> *The future is ahead, prepare for it.*
> *The present is here, live it.*
> — *Thomas S. Monson*

4. SIMPLIFY, SIMPLIFY, SIMPLIFY!

Unnecessary possessions are unnecessary burdens... There is great freedom in simplicity of living. It is those who have enough but not too much who are the happiest.

> — *Peace Pilgrim*

Since 1970, there has been a sharp rise in the number of new products. With that, consumer consumption has jumped 62%. However, as previously noted, there has not been a corresponding rise in happiness. In fact, there's been a decrease in the quality of life as measured by the Index of Social Health.

Clearly, more does not mean better. All the gizmos and gadgets meant to save time and make life simpler have made it more complex and complicated. People don't have time for simple pleasures: reading, leisurely walks, visits with family and friends. Ideally, retirement means time for such pursuits, but it takes more than time. It takes a new mindset.

When bodies and minds have been on the go for many years, slowing down and simplifying, enjoying the rewards of silence and solitude can cause anxiety. If we're not busy, feelings of being unimportant, unproductive and unneeded bubble up. With them comes a disturbing sense of emptiness, and we tend to rush to fill the void. Years ago, I gave a series of classes in which one of the assignments was to clean up, clean out and simplify the home. The following week one woman told me that she had immediately tackled the project and soon filled six big boxes. She put them in the garage and called Faith Farm to collect them. I began to congratulate her, but she stopped me. "There was a little problem," she confessed. "Faith Farm couldn't come for four days and by then I had put everything back."

It's best to ease into simplicity. Gradually eliminate the clutter from your life. Since outer reflects inner and vice-versa, you can work from outside in or inside out to simplify your life. One will affect the other. The mess on your desk, in your house, your closet, your garage is reflective of mental clutter. Get rid of what you don't need and don't use. As you bring order to your external world, you will notice an internal shift. Simplicity brings clarity and energy. You'll feel lighter, brighter, clearer.

If you choose to work from inside out, you will find that clearing your mind of nagging thoughts will naturally lead to a more orderly life. Make a list of all the things floating around in your mind that need to be attended to — the thank you letter you haven't written, the friend you haven't called in a long time, the physical exam you keep putting off. Cleaning them up one by one will ease your mind and relieve stress. It will also motivate you to create a more orderly environment.

Simplifying means getting rid of the non-essentials so you can discover, focus on and enjoy what's most valuable and fulfilling for you. That includes removing things from your life that aren't serving you well like bad habits.

5. PRIORITIZE

Action expresses priorities.
— Mahatma Gandhi

Each stage of life requires its own unique strategies. As we enter a new phase, it behooves us to stop, reflect and reassess. What's working? What's not? What is most important to you? Is that where you're expending most of your energy and time?

Priorities change at different stages of life. You may be giving time and energy to things that no longer warrant them, and not to things and people that do. In the book *Breakpoint and Beyond*, George Land and Beth Jarman explain how businesses that sailed to success on one set of strategies would fail at a certain point if they didn't revamp, re-strategize, discover and follow a whole new set of rules.

Cars are amazing vehicles and they can take us all the way from the east coast to the west coast. But if we try to get to Hawaii in a car, we'll drown. It's the same when we pass from one stage of life to another. When the territory changes, we have to change vehicles, employ a different set of tools. What worked in the past may no longer serve our purpose.

If your priorities have changed but you haven't, there's going to be a problem. When Joe retired from the Navy, one of his goals was to develop a closer relationship with his grandchildren. He invited them to participate in his hobby of building model ships. Joe addressed the children as if they were sailors under his command, was impatient when they didn't follow orders and berated them for carelessness. The kids soon lost interest in *playing* with Grandpa.

One evening, Joe's wife asked him, "What's more important to you? That ship you're working on or your grandchildren?"

"The kids of course," Joe answered indignantly.

"Then why don't you let them do it their way. It won't be perfect but they'll get better with your encouragement not your criticism. And they'll have fun. So will you."

Joe couldn't sleep that night. He had to decide whether his priority was to be in charge or have a good relationship with his grandchildren. In his heart, he wanted the latter, but he realized that it meant making some fundamental changes in his behavior. Finally he came up with a plan, and fell asleep. Right after breakfast, Joe went to the hobby shop and bought three beginner models for children. In his workroom, he set up stations for each grandchild with ship pieces, tools and glue. He called his daughter and asked her to bring the children over after school. They were reluctant to return to Grandpa's workshop but when they did, they were excited to find their own work station where they could build their own ship. They remained hesitant, however, until they noted the change in Grandpa. He was laughing, telling them not to worry about making mistakes, just have fun. That day, by gently guiding and encouraging them, Joe began a warm relationship with his grandchildren that continues to this day.

Joe is a perfect example of what happens when we don't re-evaluate our priorities. Sometimes, out of habit, we keep doing what we did before — even if it no longer serves or interests us. By the Law of Least Resistance, energy will keep moving in the same direction unless an external force acts upon it. That external force is choice. Consciously or unconsciously, we are always making choices. Everything we do is the result of a choice made on some level.

> *Life is the sum of all your choices.*
> *— Albert Camus*

Be aware of the choices you make every day. Are they life-serving? Are they taking you where you want to go? Make a list of your desires and goals and then prioritize them. Are your goals meaningful to you or based on what others think? What do you truly value most? What have you always wanted to do and why aren't you doing it? Is your focus of attention and most of your action in accord with your priorities, moving you in the direction you want to go?

If you're not happy with your life and what you're doing, it's time to choose again. Don't try to change too much at once. You'll set yourself up for disappointment, failure and stress. You'll be like the woman who cleaned out her house too fast, had an anxiety attack and put it all back. You'll have more success and much less stress if you make changes in small increments. Stress comes from trying to do too much at once or over-attention to unimportant details, neglecting what really needs to be attended to. At all ages and especially in the latter years, we do best by focusing on one thing at a time. Set your priorities and then tackle them one at a time.

6. COMPENSATE

> *All that is human must retrograde if it does not advance.*
> — *Edward Gibbon*

Just because we are not as strong or as fast as we once were does not mean that we must retreat from life, stop growing. If there is something you can't do anymore, find something else you can.

Always focus on your strengths, not your weaknesses.

This is the primary premise of positive psychology. Don't bemoan what you've lost. Build on what you've got. What are your best qualities? Your strengths? What situations/people bring out the best in you? What makes you feel creative?

One of the most difficult aspects of aging is losing strength and abilities that we've taken for granted. But even with the best of health and exercise programs, our bodies change. We may not be as fast, as strong, as tireless as we were 20, 30 or 40 years ago, but that doesn't mean we can't still do a lot of the same things.

Bill is an avid tennis player. When he noticed that he was slowing down on the court and tiring more easily, he spent an extra twenty minutes a day on the treadmill to build up endurance and took lessons to improve his placement of shots. He's now well into his seventies and still playing a good game of tennis with men considerably younger. Bill compensated for his losses by building on his core strengths — discipline and determination. In the process, he discovered new strengths. Bill turned out to be an excellent strategist and is enjoying the game more than ever before. His advice? "Don't give up on something because you can't do it as well as you could before or in the same way. There's always another way to go at a thing."

Everyone has their own unique methods of compensating. According to one urban legend...

An older woman circled the supermarket parking lot several times looking for a space. Finally she saw someone headed for her car, followed and waited patiently with her blinker on until the other woman pulled out. But a young man in a sports car raced into the spot before she could.

"How could you do that?" she yelled at him when he emerged from his car. "You saw me waiting for that space!"

"Sorry, Granny," he laughed. "That's what happens you're young and fast."

As he walked away, he heard a loud crash and crunch of metal. He turned to find that the woman had run her Mercedes into his car.

"You ran into my car on purpose," he yelled. "How could you do that?"

"Sorry, Sonny," she smiled. "That's what happens when you're old and rich."

Do an honest assessment of where you are at this time of your life. Shift your focus from what you can't do to what you can do. Know your strengths and build on them. Know yourself, when your mind is sharpest, your body strongest, and schedule your activities accordingly. Slow down. It will help you focus and increase efficiency. Take it easy. Adapt your exercise routine to your changing abilities. Do your eyes tire quickly when reading? Try talking books. Use the phone if you don't have the patience to write a letter. Use memory aids. Prepare ahead for upcoming situations. Bemoaning disabilities is a waste of time and energy. Learn to compensate for them and get on with your life.

7. PERSEVERE

It's not that I'm so smart, it's just that I stay with problems longer.
— Albert Einstein

Most successful people will tell you that it wasn't talent or brains that got them to the top of the hill so much as perseverance. They saw mistakes as learning experiences not failure. They knew that the key to success was to keep going. We grow by stretching beyond our parameters, breaking through boundaries. Every time we face a challenge, experiment, step out of our comfort zone, we build confidence whether we succeed or not! We stretch, we grow, we learn, and that is its own reward.

The race is not always to the swift... but to those who keep on running.
— Author Unknown

Mistakes are stepping stones to the right answer. We learn what works by learning what doesn't. Where would we be were it not for the perseverance of scientists and inventors? Being black in the south in the late 1800s, George Washington Carver struggled more than most. But love of his subject, purpose and perseverance led him to countless discoveries including over 300 uses for the peanut. When asked how he achieved this, he replied, "Anything will give up its secrets if you love it enough."

Great as his love was, it did not bring immediate results. Mr. Carver spent many years concentrating and probing and experimenting. Persevering. If you love something, as he did, you will naturally persevere. The trick is to persevere when something is difficult and not begetting the results desired.

Let's say you've moved to a new town or sold everything and hit the road in an RV, and it's not what you had hoped. Give things time. When I first moved to Florida in 1976, I was anxious to move back north. Everyone told me, "Give it a year." Sure enough, after a year I loved Florida and still make my home there 30 years later. Give yourself time to adjust to changes. Don't expect everything to be perfect right away. Perhaps you've taken up golf and are terrible at it. So what? If you're enjoying it, keep at it. Or perhaps you've lost some physical ability and are undergoing therapy, but not seeing the hoped for results. Be patient. Persevere. Success, fulfillment, strength, character and self-esteem come with perseverance.

8. PLAY

Youth is a perpetual intoxication; it is a fever of the mind.
— *François Duc de la Rochefoucauld*

Are you having fun? Do you find life enjoyable? If not, it's time to re-evaluate your priorities. Joy and playfulness are aspects of happiness. Play keeps us thinking and feeling young. A playful attitude is fundamental to creativity and a cheerful environment increases productivity. Children learn and develop through play, and so can we.

Some years ago when my niece was 3 years old, she answered the phone when I called my brother's house. I asked what she had been doing that day…

"This morning, I went to school and played," she said. "Then I came home and played with my friend next door. And then Conor (her brother) came home from school and we played."

"That's an awful lot of playing, Caity," I said. "Maybe it's time for you to get a job."

"Aunt Geri," she explained, "When I go to school and play, that is my job."

Make playing part of your job. Incorporate fun activities, laughter and play into your life. Go on vacation — even if it is for a day and into the next town. Do things for the pure joy of it. You will add sparkle to your life, and others will be drawn to you.

SUGGESTED READING:
Aging Well by George E. Vaillant, M.D.

MORE INFORMATION: www.realsimple.com

QUOTES TO LIVE BY:

> *There are only two ways to live your life:*
> *One is as though nothing is a miracle. The other is as if everything is.*
> *I believe in the latter.*
> — *Albert Einstein*

Chapter 6

GRATITUDE = GREAT ATTITUDE

Let us rise up and be thankful, for if we didn't learn a lot today, at least we learned a little, and if we didn't learn a little, at least we didn't get sick, and if we got sick, at least we didn't die; so, let us all be thankful.

Buddha

Gratitude is the fastest way to increase your level of happiness, and one of three qualities that happy people of all ages have and practice. The others are forgiveness and love. We've mentioned forgiveness. Love is part and parcel of everything we've talked about. It's the essence of true happiness

Stop and count your blessings for a quick fix of happiness. Gratitude has the power to change mood and perception. It pours cool water on the fiery emotions of envy, regret and greed. It reduces stress, negativity, resentment and pain. Grateful people have less illness, complaints and depression. Research has shown that people who DAILY count or record their blessings feel better about their lives, are more resilient, optimistic, enthusiastic, sleep better, have closer family ties and clearer thinking. In short…

GRATITUDE = GREAT ATTITUDE

Gratitude is far more than simply expressing appreciation. If I drop something and a stranger picks it up and hands it to me, I appreciate the act of courtesy and say thank you. But if I drop my credit card and he follows me a block to give it back, I am more than appreciative. I am thrilled. I am enriched not only by the return of the card but my brief encounter with this stranger. I am moved by his honesty and decency, my faith in mankind is restored and I am filled with a sense of peace and goodwill. I walk on with gratitude, a great attitude.

Real gratitude is laced with wonder and joy. Most of us look at a beautiful sunset and enjoy it. But how often do we feel the wonder of the little girl who ran in the house one evening and excitedly told her mother, "I didn't think purple went with orange until I saw the sunset God just made!"

> *Gratitude is happiness doubled by wonder.*
> — *G.K. Chesterton*

Gratitude is like a light switch. It turns on the light and erases darkness. With gratitude we can switch perception from problem to opportunity, from resistance to acceptance, from ending to beginning, from sickness to healing, from anger to forgiveness. Easier said than done? Not really. Find just one thing to feel truly grateful for in the midst of any situation and it is so powerful that it will overcome other emotions. Once you turn on gratitude, it keeps flowing and growing.

If you want to see a fast and positive change in your life, inject your days with abundant doses of gratitude. Don't just think about it. Write about it, talk about it. Before falling asleep, review all the good the day held and be thankful. Before getting out of bed in the morning, spend 30 seconds giving thanks for the day to come and all the potential good it holds. Every day, write down a different thing, person, experience you're grateful for. Keep the papers together and read them at the end of the month. If possible, do this with a friend or family member and the energy of gratitude will rise exponentially as you share your gifts of gratitude. Develop the habit of being thankful every day, in every situation. Be grateful for all your experiences, including problems and mistakes.

> *Every problem has a gift for you in its hands.*
> *You have the problem because you need the gift.*
> — *Richard Bach in* Jonathon Livingston Seagull

Gratitude expressed anywhere — to health, work, relationships — is like a lubricant that increases the flow of good into and through those areas. Your body loves gratitude. Move your awareness through each area of your body as you say, "Thank you." Feel the cells tingle and respond with renewed energy. Express gratitude all day long. Thank the day, the sun or the rain, thank your car, thank your home, thank the people in your life. Send a pretty card or email or leave a special message on someone's phone. You'll lift the spirits of that person as well as your own.

Just say thank you. Gratitude expressed to other people is an instant elixir that soothes hurts feelings, raises dashed hope and heals conflict. A sincere thank you to another says, "I see you, value and appreciate you." A connection is made at the soul level and both giver and receiver are blessed.

> *If the only prayer you say in your whole life is "Thank you,"*
> *that would suffice.*
> — *Meister Eckhart*

Feeling down, anxious, angry? Focus on what you're grateful for, all that's right with your life. Gratitude alters biochemistry, elevates mood, shifts perception. **For 20 seconds, smile, laugh, think**

a happy thought or feel grateful and you will change your emotional vibration.

Gratitude is fulfilling — it fills us full of joy and appreciation and love. The more we're thankful, the more we realize how much we have to be thankful for. Gratitude is like a tender, invisible hand that goes out from us and blesses everything it touches. When you approach anything with gratitude you project a great attitude and it responds to in kind.

The great medical missionary Albert Schweitzer said, "Those who thank God much are truly wealthy. So our **inner happiness depends not on what we experience but on the degree of our gratitude** to God, whatever the experience."

We have much to be thankful for but sometimes we forget. A 6th grade teacher asked her students to list what they considered the "Seven Wonders of the World." The majority of votes went to: The Pyramids of Egypt, The Taj Mahal, The Grand Canyon, The Great Wall of China, The Panama Canal, St. Peter's Basilica and The Empire State Building.

The teacher noticed that one child hadn't voted. When asked what was on her list, the girl said, "I don't have any of those things."

"Why don't you tell us what you do have," the teacher suggested. This is what was on her list:

TO HEAR and TO SEE. To which I'd add Kahlil Gibran's words: "Should you open your ears and listen, you would hear your own voice in all voices. And should you really open your eyes and see you'd behold your image in all images."

TO TOUCH: Physical affection changes bio-chemistry, releases stress, lifts depression and boosts the immune system.

TO TASTE: If you ever had to eat your words, you know they can taste more bitter than any food. When a 4 year old boy was asked what love is, he said these amazing words: "When someone loves you, the way they say your name is different. You know your name is safe in their mouth." Wouldn't it be nice if all names were safe in our mouths?

TO FEEL: People may not remember exactly what you did or what you said, but they will always remember how you made them feel.

TO LAUGH: Laughter improves mental, physical and emotional health. It stimulates the brain, releases tension and stress, can erase anger and create a bond between people. To laugh more, play more.

A little girl said to her mother, "Mommy, can I go outside and play with the boys?"

"No, honey," her mother replied. "The boys are too rough to play with."

"If I can find a smooth one, can I play with him?"

TO LOVE: When asked, "What is love?" children gave these answers:

Age 4: Love is what makes you smile when you're tired.

Age 7: When you love somebody, your eyelashes go up and down and little stars come out of you.

Age 6: Love is like a little old woman and a little old man who are still friends even after they know each other so well.

I have found that if you love life, life will love you back.
— Arthur Rubinstein

Gratitude opens our hearts and eyes. The world is seen in a brighter light. The commonplace becomes miraculous.

JUNE'S STORY

June was one of the most grateful people I ever met. There was a fairly long period of time when I saw her every week as she attended classes I gave. She always arrived a little early with a big smile, pronouncing the day 'absolutely wonderful' or some person she knew 'simply darling.' I never heard her utter a bad word about anyone.

June had all the happiness qualities we've talked about — faith, purpose, giving of one's self, kindness, a positive attitude. And she exuded gratitude. When I asked her in 2005 to let me share her story in this book, she described herself as: "an 85 year old, overweight, walker and wheelchair bound lady who has had her left leg amputated. Mentally, I am alert, outgoing and independent. Spiritually, I'm blessed, enthusiastic, productive and grateful to God."

I'm not quite sure where or when June developed her incredible attitude because her life was harder than most. Her parents divorced when she was 2 and she was sent to live with a Swedish family for the next 7 years, and then to boarding school while her mother pursued work. When June was 12, her mother remarried and it was the first time June had a normal home and family. She was elated. A year later the Depression hit. Her new dad lost his money, his business and their home.

After high school, June attended beauty school and began a 35 year career in that field. By the time she was in her early twenties, she was married. A son and two daughters followed. But June's husband was an alcoholic and eventually, they divorced. He died at the age of 47 and June acquired a real estate license to increase her income so she could raise her children.

"Once more," June says, "God provided. Into our lives like the sun came a loving, caring man willing to share responsibility in raising my children. He danced, sang songs, took us camping, cooked our meals and loved us." Together they had a baby, but June's beloved husband died suddenly of a massive heart attack when their daughter was 9.

After her husband's death and the three older children were grown, June felt she was just drifting. That was not her style, so she told her youngest it was time for an adventure. They sold everything, packed the car with some clothes and headed for Florida. Unable to use the cosmetology and real estate licenses from her home state of Michigan, June got a job at the prestigious Boca Raton Hotel and Club. She loved working there and quickly rose from cashier to Assistant Income Auditor, but there were no health benefits.

Aside from her job at the hotel, June was doing volunteer work at the Boca Raton Community Hospital. One day she saw a notice advertising a class for Unit Clerks. June was 55 at the time and wondered if she would be able to learn the medical terms, transcribe doctor's orders, spell the medications. But she signed up, passed and was hired by the hospital. Her new job included a higher salary and excellent health benefits. June worked there for 10 years, choosing the midnight shift so she would have her days free.

During that 10 years, June volunteered to teach classes at the hospital for immigrant employees, took classes at Florida Atlantic University, was active at her church and in the Artist's Guild (June was a fabulous artist and creator of stained glass). Her spiritual studies helped her through the death of her son from alcoholism.

At the urging of her children, June eventually returned to Michigan where she continued her varied studies and volunteer activities. The loss of a leg due to a blood clot necessitated her moving into a HUD sponsored apartment building with handicap facilities. There, she organized and managed the Arts and Crafts Gift Shop.

When June was 83, a cherished friend died and left her $2,000. With it, she bought a computer and took classes. To earn a little extra money and keep busy, June designed greeting cards on the computer to sell. The computer also inspired her to take a mail order writing class.

June relished life and people and sang a constant song of gratitude. She never focused on the tragedies, always on the triumphs. But her greatest heartbreak was yet to come. In 2005, at the age of 50, June's youngest daughter succumbed to a massive heart attack as her father had. June herself died peacefully and without pain in 2007. When she sent me her life story, she concluded with these words...

"I feel that I have lived a full life and accomplished much. I have learned great things and hope I have touched others. I am fortunate to still be able to function productively. I'm blessed and grateful to God. Some of the best things I've learned are: Don't let fear or lack rule you. Never hoard money. It is only a necessity to be used as a bartering tool or to share. And give generously of your time and talents."

SIMPLE HAPPINESS RULES

Be Kind
Be grateful
Smile a lot.

SUGGESTED READING: *Attitudes of Gratitude: How to Give and Receive Joy Everyday of Your Life* by M. J. Ryan

QUOTES TO LIVE BY:

To be alive, to be able to see, to walk...it's all a miracle.
I have adopted the technique of living life from miracle to miracle.

— Arthur Rubinstein

Chapter 7

PUT ON A HAPPY FACE

His face bespoke his soul.
Voltaire

Happiness is a state of mind that is not shattered or lost when things don't go right. Everyone feels upset, anxious, angry at times, but happy people know those times will pass. Even more important, they know they can learn from them. They remain at peace inside, optimistic about the future, and confident in their abilities to deal with the problem at hand.

One research project compared people who won the lottery to people who were paralyzed as the result of an accident. After the initial euphoria for the first group and despair for the second, the paralyzed group actually had higher levels of happiness than the lottery winners. They cherished what they did have, built on their strengths, rejoiced in each small sign of progress. The lottery winners, on the other hand, believed that money would solve all their problems and had such unrealistic expectations that they were consistently disappointed.

Truly happy people are not Pollyannas. They don't expect or pretend to be on top of the world every minute. They allow themselves to feel the emotions appropriate to life's various events and experiences. They welcome challenges, knowing that facing the challenge is what builds character.

Some years ago, a professional golfer, I'll call him Bill, came to me who had missed the cut in his last 7 tournaments by 1 stroke. That meant he didn't get past the preliminary round into the final tournament. I have worked with professional athletes and know they can suffer from trying too hard, freezing under pressure or feeling unworthy of great success. We did several processes to discover where Bill's block was, but he didn't have any of the typical problems.

Things had been going perfectly for Bill until this sudden, inexplicable bump in the road. Clearly, I would have to go in another direction. His childhood? Sounded idyllic. Marriage? He was happily married to his college sweetheart. The more I delved, the more perplexed I became. Bill's problem wasn't in the past, wasn't a lack of talent or self-esteem. I asked him if he could pinpoint when his golf game began slipping.

It didn't take long for Bill to realize that it was the day he started 'talking trash,' as he put it, about golf. As he explained the scenario to me, I realized that Bill had succumbed to what I call "negative by association." He was spending a lot of time with certain golfers who constantly talked about the pressure they were under to keep their sponsors, the never ending competition with friends, the threat of newcomers, getting older, losing one's edge, the trials and tribulations of travel.

The message was clear: Life is hard. You've got to pay your dues. Success is fleeting. Bad things happen to good golfers. Gradually, and unaware of what was happening, Bill began echoing the same thoughts. To be in harmony with his friends, he was taking on their attitude. He was on his way to messing up a great golf career because he was adopting the idea that life shouldn't be as easy as it had been for him. But that attitude was not serving him well, and Bill immediately grasped that.

It's difficult to maintain a positive attitude when those around us are 'talking trash,' as Bill would say. As we grow up, joy usually goes down. As children we hear the word No hundreds of times more than we hear the word Yes. Things are framed in negative terms: Don't spill your milk, don't get dirty, don't fight with your brother or sister. The older we get, the more negativity is apt to color our thinking.

No one can deny that there are atrocities in this world. Wars and famine, poverty and crime, inhumanity and injustice. Every person in this world has surely suffered pain. Getting depressed about it doesn't help anybody. Only by holding to higher ground can we bring ourselves and others up.

Imagine someone has fallen into a deep hole and can't get out. You walk by and he calls to you. You stand at the side of the hole as he pours out his terrible predicament to you. You feel so sorry for this person that you jump down and put your arms around him to give comfort. Guess what? Now there are two people stuck in the hole.

When I first moved to Florida, I took a job as the activity director of a nursing home. People would inevitably say to me, "Isn't it depressing to work there?" Frankly, it never dawned on me to look at it that way. I wouldn't have been able to do my job. How in the world could I have brought a little joy to residents' lives if I was depressed?

We have a challenge every day, every hour, every minute. Are we going to get down in the hole, wallow in negativity and pity, or stay outside where we have the potential to help others out? It isn't always easy to maintain the higher ground and sometimes it's downright impossible to lift others out of a hole, but joining them doesn't serve them or us.

Some people enjoy misery, identify with their pain. They wear suffering on their sleeves like an award, happy to share it with the world, anxious to outdo their neighbor when it comes to telling war stories. They build body and personality around their personal tragedies. The more we're exposed to such people, the more likely we are to pick up the bad habit of negativity. **Negativity is a habit and it's like quicksand — step in it and you immediately start to sink**. To help Bill regain his positive attitude, I told him this fable:

In a kingdom far away and long ago, there ruled a very cruel king. His people feared and hated him. He could have been a handsome man but his brutality had made him ugly. He was always yelling and cursing and punishing people. Scowls of hatred and anger lined his face.

One day he was looking out the window of his castle when a young maiden walked by on her way to the market. She was radiantly beautiful, smiling and singing a happy song as she passed by. He fell totally, madly in love with her. Every morning he stood by the window waiting for her to pass. The king decided he could not live without this girl, that he must have her for his wife.

The king was not a stupid man; he knew he was ugly and reviled by his people. So he called his magician, the best in the land, and told him, "Make me a handsome man, so the beautiful maiden will love and marry me."

The magician returned to the king a week later. "I have made you a mask of wax," he explained. "It will meld to your face and give you the appearance of a happy, smiling, kind man."

"That's wonderful!" cried the king.

"Ah, but this wax is very fragile" warned the magician. "So as not to appear as a mask, you must hold your face in its form or it will crack and fall off."

"How can I do that?" asked the king.

"By thinking only kind and loving, happy thoughts," the magician told him.

The king was worried about this but willing to try. So, he closed his eyes and the magician applied the mask. The king was so delighted with his new appearance that he ran into the street the very next morning, got down on his knees when the maiden approached and asked for her hand in marriage.

Since she lived outside the city limits she did not know what the king really looked like or what a vile reputation he had. She fell in love with his warm smile and kind face and said yes.

The king and the maiden were married and lived happily for several years. Whenever he was on the verge of getting angry and felt a frown forming on his face, he thought of his beautiful, sweet bride and was immediately filled with love.

The only thing that marred their relationship was that he knew he was deceiving her. He thought he would rather lose her than have her go on loving him under false pretenses. So, he called the magician and ordered him to remove the mask. That night, he entered their bedchamber and stood before his wife.

"My dearest," he said, "I can deceive you no longer. I stand before you as I really am."

"Oh, my love," she cried with delight. "What kind of game is this?"

"It is no game," he protested. "I am showing you my true face."

"Ah," she laughed. "You are posing a riddle for me, are you not?"

"No, my love. This is my real face. Can't you see the difference?"

She studied him carefully. "Oh, yes," she agreed at last. "Now I see it. For some reason, your face is even more handsome and radiant than it was this morning."

Can you guess what happened? The magician had never applied a mask. When the king closed his eyes, the magician simply used his fingers to mold the king's face into a smiling, kind countenance and told him the thoughts he needed to hold in order to maintain that expression. Later, when the magician supposedly removed the mask, the king's face retained the same kind expression he had developed naturally from thinking only good and loving thoughts. He was showing his beloved his true face — one that had been perfected by perfect thinking.

It is a challenge in this world to think only kind and loving thoughts, especially when confronted with tragedy or suffering. But if you want to make a positive difference, you must stay on higher ground. Your first reaction to something might be one of worry or condemnation. That's okay. Allow yourself to feel the feeling but don't get trapped in it. Let the emotion subside and then choose to raise your thinking to a higher level.

That's how Bill turned his life around. We developed a little code that helped him remember the goal: HTHT. It means *Hold The Highest Thought*. **Negative thoughts may grab your attention, just don't let them keep it.** Think the highest thought possible in a given situation and hold onto it. There will be bumps in the road, detours and even occasional breakdowns. But often our greatest triumphs come out of those trials. So, don't despair.

Don't let negativity be your master. Put on a happy face and Hold The Highest Thought.

SUGGESTED READING: *As A Man Thinketh* by James Allen

QUOTES TO LIVE BY:

He who cannot change the very fabric of his thought will never be able to change reality, and will never, therefore, make any progress...
— *Anwar Sadat*

Chapter 8

ATTITUDE =ALTITUDE

Could we change our attitude, we should not only see life differently, but life itself would come to be different.

Katherine Mansfield

DON'T SKIP THIS CHAPTER! I know. So much has been written and said about the power of positive thinking that you assume you know what's coming, don't believe it; it's trite, hasn't helped you. Unfortunately *positive thinking* has become a bit of an overworked cliché. We can't even be sure what it means anymore. Is it magical thinking? Does it deny obvious problems and *pretend* they don't exist? Is it robotic repetition of affirmations? Hopefully, this chapter will answer those questions. So, let's start fresh, and talk about a positive *attitude*. Positive thinking may come and go but attitude is how we choose to look at life, the filter we perceive things through, our fundamental mindset.

These questions reveal your basic attitude about life:

Is your motivation to praise or find fault?
Do you worry a lot?
Are you opinionated and judgmental?

Do you let little stuff cause big upsets?

Are you grateful for what you have or envious of what you lack?

Are you inclined to forgive or hold grievances?

Are you cynical and sarcastic?

Are you an optimist or a pessimist?

Are you cooperative or aggressive?

Do you expect the worst or the best?

On a scale of 1 – 10 (10 being best) how satisfied are you with life?

What do your answers say about you and your attitude? Do you like this person? Is this the person you want to be? If you are still not sure about the attitude you project, start listening to yourself. How many positive things do you say? How many critical, negative things?

The following statements reveal your basic attitude about aging. Do you agree or disagree?

As you age, you are less useful.

Things get worse as you get older.

It's all downhill after age _____ (fill in the blank).

People who disagree with statements like these tend to live up to 7½ years longer than their negative counterparts. Negative images about aging often turn into self-fulfilling prophesies. People who hold them are more likely to become frail and suffer memory loss. On the other hand...

OPTIMISTIC PEOPLE

Have stronger immune systems
Are 77 % less likely to die of heart attack or stroke than pessimists
Are less stressed, more resilient
Age slower

Live longer
Less likely to become frail.

Optimistic people don't deny the clouds; they carry umbrellas. But they do look for the silver lining. They know there is always another way to look at a situation. They see obstacles as challenges, detours as adventures, and problems as learning opportunities. Negativity drains people of energy, confidence and determination, making them more likely to give up in the face of obstacles.

The block of granite which was an obstacle in the pathway of the weak,
became a stepping-stone in the pathway of the strong.
— Thomas Carlyle

Thoughts send chemicals through the brain and body that evoke physical and emotional sensations. Positive thoughts release serotonin which makes us feel good, aids memory and prevents brain damage. Negative thoughts are toxic. They release chemicals that are harmful to the immune system, deplete energy, speed aging and damage brain cells. A negative attitude can literally make you sick.

Pessimism is hazardous to your health!

It is estimated that at least 75% of illness originates in the mind. Prolonged negativity leads to depression which releases more toxic hormones that further weaken the immune system and lower the body's ability to fight disease. Today, stress is the major cause of illness in the industrialized world, but by 2020 it is believed depression will be.

No one is *up* all the time, but people with a positive attitude bounce back faster. Some people are luckier than others in that they were raised in a positive environment or are genetically inclined to have an optimistic nature. But the fact remains that your thoughts are the foundation of your attitude, and you — you alone —

are responsible for your thoughts. What happens *to* a person only affects his happiness level about 10%. What's important is how we react to what happens to us. Reaction springs from attitude.

A positive attitude can be developed. Since we can change our thoughts, we can change our attitude. And a change in attitude has dramatic effects. An amazing example of this was demonstrated in 1979 by Harvard researcher Ellen Langer and her associates. Healthy men over the age of 75 spent a week at a retreat where everything was designed to reflect a time of life 20 years earlier. Television and radio shows from 20 years before played. Newspapers and magazines of that period were available. The participants were asked to think, talk and act 20 years younger. By the end of the week, the men looked, behaved and felt younger. Even their hearing and vision improved!

Kinesiology has proven that thoughts can strengthen or weaken a body. A positive attitude contributes to health, emotional well-being and relationships. Negativity repels people as surely as happiness attracts them.

> *A loving person lives in a loving world.*
> *A hostile person lives in a hostile world;*
> *everyone you meet is your mirror.*
> — *Ken Keyes, Jr.*

Thoughts activate emotions, and emotions have corresponding physical sensations. If you're in a good mood, you literally feel good and vice versa. Just anticipating a positive event can ease stress and make you feel better. The expression on your face affects how you feel. Smiling activates a 'feel good' physiological response. In his book *Mind Sculpture*, Ian Robertson writes, "the brain circuits which control particular facial expression are closely linked to the brain circuits for the experiencing of these emotions themselves."

In his classic book, *Man's Search for Meaning*, Viktor E. Frankl describes life as a prisoner in Nazi concentration camps. Though he and his fellow prisoners all experienced the same depravity, and were stripped of everything considered necessary and meaningful in this world, he noted a basic difference among them. Attitude. In his own words...

"...everything can be taken from a man but one thing: the last of the human freedoms — to choose one's attitude in any given set of circumstances, to choose one's own way." He also writes, "Man is not fully conditioned and determined but rather determines himself whether he gives in to conditions or stands up to them. In other words, man is ultimately self-determining. Man does not simply exist but always decides what his existence will be, what he will become in the next moment."

How exciting! We determine what we will be in the next moment. Not the weather, family, government, bank account. Us. You. Me. **WE DETERMINE WHAT WE WILL BE IN THE NEXT MOMENT.** William James put it in these words...

> *The greatest discovery of my generation is that*
> *a human being can alter his life by altering his attitude.*

It is easy to echo platitudes about positive thinking. The challenge is to incorporate them into the way one lives. There are lots of guidelines for doing that, but before any lasting change can be made, you must ask yourself a pivotal question. Do you really want to have a more positive outlook and attitude? Maybe I should put that another way... **Are you willing to let go of your negativity?**

We do what we do because there is a payoff in it. My mother's nursing home was not far from our condo and one day my husband stopped to see her while he was riding his bike. In the course of their conversation, my mother confessed that she had been depressed when she first entered the nursing home. "And there are some benefits to that," she told Ron. "They give you extra ice cream." She saw the payoff in being depressed, but she asked herself the next important question: Was the depression worth it? Was it getting her what she really wanted? No! She told Ron that what she wanted was to be an inspiration to the other residents. She wanted people to enjoy being around her, not feel sorry for her. That was more important to her than ice cream — and trust me, my mother loved ice cream. So, she *chose* to accept her circumstances and make the best of them. And she did. She was a livewire at the nursing home, spreading love and laughter. Nurses and patients alike adored her.

People express their negativity in different ways: cynicism, judgment, criticism, complaining, hopelessness, anger. At the bottom of it is a sense of victimization. "People, life, my body is not giving me what I want!" Ironically, it is. By dwelling on the negative, we nurture it, increasing its vibratory power, thus drawing more of it into our lives.

FOCUS OF ATTENTION CREATES!

Your mind thinks you want more of what you dwell on, talk about, worry about — and gives it to you! Focusing on something virtually injects it with energy. It grows bigger and stronger. You may have a valid reason for being depressed or negative. It doesn't really matter what that is. What matters is whether you want to keep your grievance or anger or depression. Before you can really let it go, you need to ask yourself...

1. WHAT'S THE PAYOFF IN MY BEING NEGATIVE? We all learned very early on that there are benefits to being sick. We got to stay home from school, eat ice cream, receive extra attention and maybe even a present. You may believe that negativity...

Gets you attention and sympathy;
Is a display of power, a way of controlling others.

Or, you may be using a negative attitude…
To express anger;
To make others feel guilty for your unhappiness;
To protect yourself from disappointment;
To drive people away, separate yourself from others;
As an excuse not to change, grow, accept challenges.

On cruise ships, we invariably meet some people who think everything is wonderful and others who find fault with everything. They are on the same ship, eating the same food, seeing the same shows. The difference obviously is not in the nature of the experience but in the nature of the experiencer. If something goes wrong, a port must be bypassed, the optimists are likely to see it as part of the adventure. The pessimists are more likely to see it as spoiling the whole cruise.

The focus of positive people is outward. What's new and exciting? What can I learn? Who can I meet? What can I offer? The focus of negative people is inward. What do I need? What can I get? How can I get it? Positive people have a sense of inner fulfillment. Good experiences are icing on the cake. Negative people have a sense of inner lack. They want external events, objects, people to fulfill them.

Constant complainers are aggressive and demanding of attention. They vent negativity because they think it's a display of power, especially on a cruise ship where the crew bends over backward to please them. This is one place they can be sure their negativity will get results, and that makes them feel superior. The same thing happens in hospitals and nursing homes.

I recall a gentleman in the nursing home where I worked who had had a stroke and was unable to move his left side. His speech was halting and garbled. He yelled most of the day, demanding insignificant things. We assumed he had always been difficult because most people become more of what they always were as they age — unless they consciously decide to change. In this case though, the patient had not been a demanding, complaining person. At a care meeting, his wife told us he had started his own company, built it into a great success, was respected and loved by his employees. He had had a great sense of humor and a positive, can-do attitude. *What happened?*

This man believed he had lost everything. No longer could he control a thriving business, direct hundreds of people, eat in the best restaurants, jog around the lake each morning. He felt powerless. Bossing the nurses and aides around was the only way he thought he could exert the authority and power that had been his driving force.

I went into his room later that day as he was berating an aide. I asked her to leave and sat down next to him. I took his hand in mine, looked in his eyes and told him that I knew what a successful and well-loved man he had been. His eyes filled with tears at the memory.

"Would you like to be loved and appreciated again?" I asked. He nodded. Then I addressed the crucial question. "Is your behavior getting you what you want?"

This man broke down and sobbed. As he calmed down, I explained that I understood why he was behaving the way he did, but clearly it wasn't making him or anyone else happy. He was growing more miserable by the day. The people who took care of him did not like or respect him. "And," I added, "I don't think you like and respect yourself right now either."

His behavior changed from that moment on. It was as if we had called his bluff and thus given him permission to give up the charade. As the staff noted the change in him, they became warmer and more attentive. As his overall attitude and interaction with people improved, so did his health. Several months later, he had recovered enough to continue his care and therapy at home.

So, the second question is...

2. IS THE PAYOFF WORTH THE PRICE? Is your negativity getting you what you really want? You may think anger, complaining and criticism bring rewards, but they are short-lived rewards. Look at the big picture. People don't like negative people! They resent the attacks and manipulation. They don't like to be subjected to the heavy, toxic energy that surrounds chronic complainers. Negative people are a burden and everyone else is tired of trying to lift them up!

If you're chronically negative, you have to face some harsh facts. No one really likes you and you're not too crazy about yourself. Your negative expectations have turned into self-fulfilling prophesies. Admit that your attitude and behavior are destroying what you truly want — happiness and love. Is what you're doing worth the price you're paying? How long are you going to bet on a horse that has no chance of winning?

In trying to get our own way, we should remember
that kisses are sweeter than whine.
— *Author Unknown*

* * * * * *

Before continuing, let's go back to the man in the nursing home who had a stroke. He illustrates that positive people can become negative just as negative ones can become positive. That doesn't happen easily but a series of setbacks or losses, prolonged illness and chronic pain can lead to depression. If that happens to you or someone you know, seek help.

SUGGESTED READING: *Man's Search for Meaning,*
Viktor E. Frankl

QUOTES TO LIVE BY:

> *Mind is the Master-power that molds and makes,*
> *And Man is Mind, and evermore he takes*
> *The tool of Thought, and shaping what he wills,*
> *Brings forth a thousand joys, a thousand ills.*
> *He thinks in secret and it comes to pass:*
> *Environment is but his looking glass.*
> *— James Allen*

Chapter 9

ATTITUDE ADJUSTMENT

Even a thought, even a possibility can shatter us and transform us.

Friedrich Nietzsche

Age plays a small role in liveliness after 55. By then our personalities are well established. Without conscious choice and effort, we tend to become more of what we always were.

To improve is to change; to be perfect is to change often.

— Winston Churchill

People don't always know or won't admit they're negative. They think the world needs to change, not them. But remember, the world is our mirror. It reflects what's in our minds. You've heard me say this before but it bears repeating: **YOUR BRAIN FINDS WHAT YOU'RE LOOKING FOR.** Start really paying attention to your thoughts and the words you speak. Listen to the way you talk about yourself, your life, other people and the world. Your brain looks for people and experiences to match your words.

I like to think of the brain as a magnificent factory with trillions of willing workers ready and anxious to do our bidding. But if not given clear orders, the workers run the same old mental machinery and fire up the same old thought patterns. You are the

Commander in Chief. The workers await your orders. What do you want to do? What's your purpose? Where do you want to go? What do you intend to create today?

Ask yourself every day and all day: **WHAT AM I LOOKING FOR?** Change what you're looking for and you'll change what you find.

The words we think, read and speak tell our mental workers what to produce. Volunteers were exposed to positive and negative words about aging prior to taking memory tests. When the tests were preceded by negatives about aging, the participants had much lower scores than when positive words about aging preceded the tests.

Words spoken aloud have a stronger vibration and evoke a response in others as well as within ourselves. Contrary to the old saying, "Sticks and stones can break my bones but words can never hurt me," negative words, your own or someone else's, can have devastating and lasting effects. We identify with the verbal labels our parents, teachers, peers cast upon us. The more positive words children hear, the more likely they are to grow up with self-esteem and a positive outlook. Certain words resonate good feelings.

POWER WORDS: wonderful, excellent, terrific, appreciate, love, magnificent, beautiful, perfect, great, awesome.

Our words and the subjects we dwell on reveal us. In a sense, we are characters in a story — and we're the author! The things we say tell the world who we are, what we are, the theme of our existence. If you want to change your life, you have to change your story.

WHAT'S YOUR STORY?

Our stories are the filter through which we perceive ourselves and the world. Your life story is composed of your strongest memories and beliefs, woven with your emotions, disposition, character and behavior. Your story is your reality. How do you describe you, the main character? What are the overriding and recurring themes of your story? Where is the plot headed?

Most of our thoughts, feelings and actions are reruns of what we thought, felt and did yesterday and the day before and so on — all reinforcing our story and self-image. The more we think a particular thought, the stronger the neural pattern, the faster it fires in the brain. The brain follows the path of least resistance. It continually triggers the neural patterns used the most. So, negative thinking breeds more negative thinking and the negative neural network is strengthened. That means that if you've held a negative attitude or perception for a long time and suddenly decide to change it, your positive thoughts are going to be like a 90 pound weakling going up against Mr. Universe. That doesn't mean attitudes can't be changed.

We can always rewrite our story. After all, we're the author. First, we need to pay attention to the story we're telling ourselves right now. What are your thinking about, feeling right now? Sadly, it is estimated that the great majority of people's thoughts and self talk is negative. Negativity includes fear, stress, worry, guilt, anger, criticism of self and others. Are you presently telling yourself a story of fatigue, anxiety, impatience, irritation?

Your subconscious hears everything you think and say, and takes it as literal truth. It doesn't have the ability to sift and sort, rationalize or reject. And it has no sense of humor whatsoever. What you say is what the subconscious gets. If you frequently put yourself down, you reinforce a negative self-image on the deepest level. And behavior corresponds to the deepest beliefs we hold about ourselves.

For real and lasting change to be made, it must be made on the subconscious level. The conscious mind programs the subconscious via pictures, words, thoughts and actions. So, you can start to reprogram your subconscious right now by taking control of your thoughts, behavior and the spoken word.

Negative neural pathways will weaken and positive ones will be established if you consistently shift attention from negative thoughts to positive ones. But this is important: **Don't deny the negative thought. Look at it, and choose against it**. Choose a thought that will give you a sense of harmony and peace. By holding fast to that thought, you can undo negative subconscious patterns of belief. You can rewire your brain and establish new neural connections. A happy environment and rewarding yourself will speed progress in establishing change.

Suppose there is a person you don't like. Whenever her name comes up, critical judgments immediately follow. You don't really like how they make you feel so you decide to see if you can change your brain. Next time that person's name comes up, the negative judgments follow but you consciously choose to shift your attention to a kind or compassionate thought about that person. As you continue holding the higher thought, the negative thought pattern weakens. It loses its charge. Eventually, when that woman's name comes up, the new perception will fire first and strongest.

The brain is plastic, changing and reshaping with every thought and experience we have. This was dramatically illustrated by an experiment NASA did a while ago. To help astronauts respond to the upside down world of space, goggles were designed that inverted everything. After wearing the goggles for several weeks, the astronauts began seeing the upside down world as right side up. Their brains had changed and were automatically making the necessary adjustment.

It takes approximately 3 - 4 weeks to make or break a habit. During that time you can literally rewire your brain by replacing negative thoughts with positive ones. The more you think, speak and visualize the positive, the faster the brain will re-configure. In *Train Your Mind Change Your Brain*, Sharon Begley writes, "The actions we take can literally expand or contract different regions of the brain... The brain can change as a result of the thoughts we have." Think of your mind as a garden and watch what you put in it. If you fill it with trash, don't nurture and water it, ugly weeds will grow wild and your garden won't be very pretty. Thoughts are living things. Stop feeding the nasty ones and they'll die. Weed them out and plant the ideas, images and feelings you want to flourish in your mental garden.

What are you watching, listening to, reading? Your subconscious is paying attention even if you're not. Notice how you feel before and after you read the newspaper, watch the evening news or listen to a friend complain. When your mood suddenly shifts from up to down, what words or action preceded that? Remember the song "Happy Talk" from South Pacific? To keep your spirits up, keep talking happy talk. When people ask how you are, don't respond with a weak, "Fine." Answer with one of the power words. Say in a strong voice, "Great! Terrific! Wonderful!"

> One day a man was going to visit his mother in a nursing home. An elderly man was in the hallway, slumped over in a wheel chair.
>
> "How are you?" asked the visitor as he passed by.
>
> The old man smiled radiantly and replied, "I am wonderful. My body is not doing too well. But I am wonderful."

Is it any surprise that the visitor stopped to spend time with that man and a friendship was born? Positive words, smiling and laughing can instantly lift you out of negativity and change your outlook. As a bonus, other people will love to be around you!

The only disability in life is a bad attitude.

— *Scott Hamilton*

CHANGING YOUR MIND

Most of what goes on in the brain is unconscious. But conscious experience and thought program the unconscious. Since the unconscious can't tell the difference between a real and imagined experience, we can also use imagination to change the brain. Repeating the same words or images for up to 30 days can create new neural patterns thereby changing the way you think, feel and act.

Just before you fall asleep and for about 30 minutes after you awaken, the conscious guard to the gate of your unconscious is on idle. These are the best times to directly program your subconscious with the thoughts and attitudes you want to adopt. So, fall asleep and wake up with good thoughts and intentions, positive affirmations and visualizations.

1. AFFIRMATIONS. Affirmations are thoughts you want to 'make firm' in your mind. By repeating them regularly throughout the day, you are weaving them into your brain. A nun whose eyesight was failing, began repeating throughout the day, "Every time I blink my eyes, they will focus accurately like the lens of a camera." In a couple of weeks, her eyesight improved dramatically.

Yes, there was a trick to it — she really believed what she said! Some people try to use affirmations as magic and hope their lives will automatically change. **Affirmations must be backed by**

belief to succeed. I have known people to repeatedly affirm being thin as they continued to eat the same fattening foods. They were setting up a conflict within their mind. The subconscious simply didn't believe their *thin* words.

As affirmations take root, they push the negative thoughts they are replacing up and out. The opposition doesn't go quietly. It puts on a little show to win you back. Don't fall for it. One of my students once complained to me, "As soon as I started affirming prosperity, my car broke down and repairs cost $500! I'm worse off than before." It's almost as if the subconscious tests us. It's trying to find out which thought we really believe. The way to convince the subconscious is to maintain the positive thought *in the face of contrary evidence*. Hold fast to your new thought, reinforce it with actions and bolster it with faith.

Since the subconscious doesn't understand time, affirmations should be based in the present and not in the future. State your declarations in positive and absolute terms. Make them precise, easy to remember and repeat. A popular affirmation is, "Every day, in every way, I'm getting better and better."

2. VISUALIZATION. The mind thinks primarily in images so it is best programmed with pictures. Consistently visualize what you want, imagine having and experiencing it. Paint a clear, precise picture of what you desire in your mind. Hold the image until it becomes energized — reinforced with physical and emotional sensations. *Feel* the reality of experiencing what you envision. In such a manner, you become a magnet, drawing what you picture to you.

Visualizations have been proven to help restore health and strength. The nervous system can't tell the difference between a real and imagined experience. Both cause the same chemistry in the body and light up the same areas of the brain. Spending at least 20 minutes a day visualizing healing has had positive effects in one month and sometimes less. The more you practice, the faster the results.

Fix your eyes on perfection and
You make almost everything speed towards it.
— *William Ellery Channing*

3. SMILE, SMILE, SMILE. Psychologist Paul Ekman who extensively studied faces said, "What we discovered is that expression alone is sufficient to create marked changes in the autonomic nervous system." Smiling has a physiological affect. It sends a message to your brain that everything is okay and you immediately start to feel better. A smile also affects your voice. It makes you sound good as well as look good. The subconscious gets the message that all is well. Your outlook and behavior are affected. Always answer the phone with a smile.

4. SHARE. We have the most amazing power: we can make other people smile and laugh. Lifting other people's spirits is the fastest way to raise your own. Your kind words and compliments can change someone's day, perhaps their life.

Kind words can be short and easy to speak but
Their echoes are truly endless.
— *Mother Theresa*

Be quick with smiles, compliments and kindness. Give generously of yourself. Your self-esteem and confidence will rise. Websites like www.volunteermatch.com can lead you to volunteer opportunities in your area.

5. ENVIRONMENT. Environment also affects mood. If you come home to a messy house, a sink overflowing with dirty dishes, a desk piled high with unopened mail, your spirits will take a nose dive. A positive environment is uplifting. It helps you relax and release stress. Determine what gives you peace and then set out to create that in your home and workplace. Lighting, colors, pictures, flowers and music affect emotions. Choose ones that make you feel good.

We'll discuss the effects of exercise and meditation on attitude in coming chapters.

* * * * * *

Negative emotions like anger and fear give us a jolt of energy and it is possible to become addicted to them for that reason. It's the most alive some people ever feel. But it is still negative energy and the long-term affect is dangerous. Like alcohol, it makes you feel better for a little while but takes a terrible toll.

SUGGESTED READING: *Train Your Mind Change Your Brain* by Sharon Begley

QUOTES TO LIVE BY:

> *Attitudes are contagious. Is yours worth catching?*
> — *Author Unknown*

HAPPY DAYS

1. START AND END THE DAY WITH GRATITUDE.

2. CHOOSE YOUR PURPOSE FOR THE DAY. What are you looking for?

3. EXPECT THE BEST. Face the day with optimism and enthusiasm. Look for the good in people and situations.

4. BE OPEN and ACCEPTING. Be flexible. Go with the flow. If things don't go your way, laugh, smile, adapt.

5. EXERCISE. A leisurely walk if nothing else.

6. GROW. Spend time studying and learning. Explore, experiment, take a risk, try something new.

7. SOCIALIZE. Enjoy the company of family and friends.

8. FORGIVE. Did someone cut you off on the highway, say an unkind word? Let it go. It isn't worth giving up your peace of mind.

9. REACH OUT. Forget yourself for a little while and do something for someone else.

10. RELAX. Take little breaks during the day to relax and refresh yourself. Treasure solitude and silence.

11. LAUGH A LOT! Laughter is good for body, brain and mood.

12. HTHT: Put on a happy face and **HOLD THE HIGHEST THOUGHT.**

Chapter 10

E-MOTION = ENGERGY IN MOTION

When dealing with people, remember you are not dealing with creatures of logic, but creatures of emotion.

Dale Carnegie

Thoughts are low vibrations of energy. The more you believe in or focus on a thought, the more it vibrates. When the vibratory rate becomes strong enough, it can literally be felt in the body. That's what we know as emotion or what I call e-motion, energy in motion.

As emotions move through the body, they stimulate physiological responses. And those responses initiate action. The progression is…

THOUGHT sparks **EMOTION** sparks **ACTION**

Since thought is at the root of emotion and action, a change of thought evokes a change in feelings and behavior. But that's not always easy to do. Emotions are much stronger vibrations of energy than thoughts. Once they're running full force, they easily overpower rational thinking.

The primary emotions are happiness, sadness, fear, anger and disgust. A multitude of other emotions spring from them. To name a few: happiness breeds enthusiasm; fear is the father of anxiety, and sadness is the precursor to depression. An ongoing emotion becomes a mood. Emotions and moods change the chemical composition of the brain and body. As you know from earlier chapters, happiness has a beneficial affect on the body-mind. It strengthens the immune system and improves brain function. Happy people are better able to cope with stress, deal with and solve problems.

Negative emotions have the opposite affect. They release harmful chemicals in the body and brain, and weaken the immune system. Studies found a 35% decrease in blood flow and a release of stress hormones just from watching scary movies. Horror movies evoked negative emotions and narrow mindedness.

The word emotion comes from the Latin word emotere which means to move out. As vibrations of energy, emotions that aren't allowed to move through and out of the body-mind get stuck inside. They form knots and blocks physiologically and psychologically. They build up and eventually blow up. They blow mature, rational thought right out the window.

Picture a basketball. If you put just the right amount of air in it, it will bounce perfectly. Add a little more air and the ball will still function but not perfectly. With too much bounce, it becomes uncontrollable. Keep adding air without releasing any and the ball will eventually explode. It's the same with our energy field.

Imagine that you are a ball of energy and perfectly balanced. A little more energy is impressed — pressed in. If you express — press it out — you will regain balance. If you repress the energy — press it back in — your equilibrium will be disturbed. If you keep repressing instead of expressing energy, your energy field will become deformed. The effects will be exhibited in your body, thoughts and emotions. Repressed energy may manifest as illness, chronic pain or emotional disturbance.

Most people don't have any problem expressing positive energy. We laugh, we cry tears of joy, we sing, we dance. We let our joy out. But unfortunately, we learn at an early age that certain emotions are bad, wrong, unacceptable. Those are the ones we start repressing. And, since my emotions are a reflection of me, I conclude that there must be something wrong with me. As we grow up, we actively try to deny what we have come to think of as our bad emotions. All this does is build up a stronger and more toxic backload of emotional energy. Eventually, it can cause mental, emotional and physical breakdown.

Life is not without pain and suffering, struggle and disappointment. Denying natural emotional responses, refusing to acknowledge and express our feelings doesn't make them go away. They get buried inside. Over time, more repressed emotion gets shoved down and we end up with an emotional monster in the closet. As the monster grows, so does fear of confronting it. First we close the door, refuse to look at it. After a while, the monster makes some noise so we lock the door. As the noise grows louder, we barricade the door. Soon we're living in constant fear that the monster will escape and destroy our life. But it already has.

Repressed energy unconsciously dominates us. Locking emotions inside and shutting down emotional outlets does one of two things. Either we can't feel anything any more, become apathetic and even emotionally catatonic, or we become super-sensitive, our emotions boiling just below the surface ready to erupt at any moment.

What if we opened the door and let the monster out? Emotions are vibrations of energy, neither right nor wrong, although the means by which they are expressed can be good or bad, helpful or harmful. Our greatest enemy is our own self-condemnation. We need to accept and express our feelings in non-destructive ways. Repressed energy can so distort perception that we don't experience what is actually happening in the present. It' like looking at the world through Vaseline covered eyeglasses, and having cotton stuffed in our ears. We project the past on the present, and totally misinterpret what we see and hear.

When we consciously choose to release our feelings without attacking ourselves or anyone else, we deflate the monster. We regain the energy that went into holding the closet door closed, and reclaim the part of ourselves we had rejected. The following process is one way to do that. You can get in touch with your repressed energy by thinking about issues or people that upset you. Facial expression, physical sensations and music can also be used to stimulate emotion. Fatigue, for instance, arouses feelings of impatience, anxiety, irritability. Some music stirs deep feelings of sadness. Develop awareness of your emotional triggers. They're tapping into hidden energy that needs to be discharged. To stay clear, try to do the Healing Feelings process whenever someone or something disturbs you.

HEALING FEELINGS

1. Find a private place where you won't be disturbed.

2. Lie down, breathe deeply and relax your whole body. (See relaxation meditation in Chapter 13)

3. Focus on the disturbing situation. Let the emotion rise. Say, "I am willing to feel this feeling." Keep repeating that to yourself as you breathe deeply. Stay relaxed and open.

4. Watch your body as you allow the emotional energy to flow freely through it. In your mind, describe the energy. How does it feel? Where is it located? What does it look like? What color is it? Keep breathing deeply as you observe the nature and movement of the energy.

5. Pay attention to any areas that are resisting the feeling, tightening up, feeling tense. Breathe into those areas as you command them to open up and let go.

6. Say, "This is just energy that wants to move out. I am willing to feel this and I am willing to let it go." Become one with the feeling and ride it out of your body with the breath.

There will likely be some type of physical or emotional reaction. Parts of your body might twitch or tingle. You could start perspiring. You may wish to talk out loud, cry, sigh, scream. It's energy moving. Let it happen. Don't fight it. After a little while, you will feel a deep shift and sense of relief. Following the release, you may feel lighter and energized or you could feel tired, the relaxing fatigue that follows a good work out. Listen to your body. Allow a period of adjustment.

SUGGESTED READING:

Molecules of Emotion by Candace Pert

QUOTES TO LIVE BY:

To give vent now and then to his feelings, whether of pleasure or discontent, is a great ease to a man's heart.

— *Francesco Guicciardini*

Chapter 11

ANGER

You will not be punished for your anger, you will be punished by your anger.
Buddha

Anger, one of the most destructive emotions, has many faces—irritation, impatience, road rage, resentment to mention a few. As a primitive brain function, anger arouses primal emotions. It has harmful biological effects and distorts perception.

Let's face it, we all have hot button issues. Those are areas we hold repressed anger around. Someone might say something totally innocuous, but the words could be like dynamite to us because of past experiences. Telling people what to do often ignites a hostile response because it arouses rebellious feelings we had as children when we had to do what we were told.

Anger triggers are usually rooted in childhood. So is the way we express it. We tend to go into a self-protective, non-thinking state and revert to childlike behavior. We may scream, cry, throw things, verbally or physically attack. I'm sure you've seen mature adults lose it if someone breaks in line in front of them, or cuts them off on the highway. By understanding anger and what causes it, we can deal with it maturely.

CAUSES OF ANGER

Anger and stress are closely related. They're primal reactions to harm or deprivation. When a person feels endangered in any way, brain centers go into warfare mode. Feelings of rage and hostility flood the body-mind in preparation for battle. People who are angry all the time are in a constant psychological and physical attack state.

The greatest common universal cause of anger is lack of reciprocation, feeling we have given more than we received. Cooperation and reciprocation are necessary to successfully living in a social environment. Being taken advantage of upsets the balance. An angry response is often an attempt to punish or control others. If we can make people feel guilty enough, they'll conform to our will and give us what we want.

Although anger is considered one of the primary emotions, it can also be secondary, arising to hide other emotions. Rather than feel helpless, guilty or sad we might choose to be antagonistic. Rather than confront fear of rejection, abandonment, betrayal, we might choose the pseudo power of anger. Remember the businessman who had a stroke? He was using anger to overcome feelings of helplessness and grief at his condition.

Due to the rush of adrenalin, some people associate anger with power. Anger may give the illusion of power but it is actually a sign of weakness, losing control. Some may argue that anger can be constructive, but that's an oxymoron. Anger in itself is always destructive BUT the energy in it can be transformed to positive action. It is not the anger but the action generated that is constructive. The purpose of anger in and of itself is to destroy. And that's what it does. Attacking never resolves situations. It always makes them worse. Anger weakens the body-mind and ruins relationships.

The next time you're angry, notice what happens to you. You release adrenaline and your heart rate and blood pressure increase. Breathing becomes rapid and shallow. Muscles tense, face flushes. Anger has a poisonous affect on your whole being and increases the risk of heart disease.

To regain control, remember that you have a choice. You are having the anger and you can let it go. Think of it as a criminal who breaks into your house and takes over everything. It says, "You, your rational mind, are no longer in control. I own you. I rule you. I can destroy you and everything you have." That's anger and that's what it can do. Just remember — you put the gun in its hand. All the power it has, you gave it. And you can take it back.

There is a split second before an urge in the brain sparks a physical reaction. Considering the tremendous speed of thought, a lot can happen in that time. During that instant we can change our minds, decide not to act upon the initial stimulus. In that instant, we can choose another perception and thereby trigger another reaction. We can claim power instead of losing it.

Since it is impossible to hold two opposing thoughts at the same time, the antidote to anger is to change your focus of attention. Concentrate on courage, patience, humor, understanding, gratitude. Anything positive will diffuse the anger. But remember the 20 second rule. You have to *Hold The Highest Thought*, the new perception, for 20 seconds before the emotional vibration changes.

There are certain universal themes to people's anger. A sense of entitlement, unrealistic expectations, desire to dominate and control, projection of guilt. The important thing to remember is that it is our own thinking that causes anger, and we can change our thinking. The sooner you catch anger rising, the easier it is to control. After a certain point, anger controls you, not vice-versa.

You will not be able to think straight. Arguing with an angry person is like arguing with a drunk. Their emotions scream so loudly that they can't think clearly much less hear or understand you.

ANGER MANAGEMENT

Anger is short-lived madness.
— Horace

1. STEP AWAY. As soon as you feel yourself losing control, move! Get away from the anger sparking situation. Take a walk, cool off. Relax, breathe deeply, let the emotions subside. Detach. Be objective. Let your rational brain be heard.

2. WHAT HAPPENED? Who/what triggered your anger? Be specific about the trigger, but know that the trigger is not the cause. It just activated what was already there. The greater the anger, the bigger the storehouse of repressed energy behind it.

He who angers you conquers you.
— Elizabeth Kenny

Learn to identify the early warning signs of anger. What starts as a slight annoyance can easily erupt into a full blown rage attack. The sooner you catch it, the easier it is to handle.

3. WHAT EMOTIONS ARE BEHIND THE ANGER? Identify the specific feelings caused by the incident. If something was lost or taken from you, you're feeling lack, insecurity. If you did something wrong, you're feeling inadequate or guilty. If your anger is in response to being taken advantage of, you may be feeling used or helpless. Fear rises faster than any other emotion and precedes anger. What are you afraid of?

Anger producing situations in the present awaken feelings of insecurity or guilt or fear from the past. The anger is a defense against feeling those feelings. But that's what needs to be addressed and released. Nothing from the past can have power over you now unless you let it.

4. WHAT THOUGHTS ARE AT THE ROOT OF THOSE FEELINGS? That's what's really upsetting you, the thoughts behind the emotion. Negative judgments about ourselves and other people spark anger. If you were embarrassed and felt humiliated, you may be thinking that you're a fool or incompetent. What negative self-talk are you listening to? Refusing to acknowledge that our thoughts cause our feelings, not something external, leaves us powerless. Frustration and anger escalate.

ANGER EXERCISE

WRITE: I am angry at _____(1)_____

because _____(2)_____.

That makes me feel_____(3)_____.

My feelings are based on these thoughts:

_____(4)_____

_____, _____.

EXAMPLE: I am angry at (1) the government because (2) they want to mess with Social Security. That makes me feel (3) worried about my future, fearful of not having enough money when I retire, helpless against the powers that be. Those feelings are based on these thoughts/beliefs: (4) I am not safe. I will not have what I need to be safe in the future. I'm helpless, there is nothing I can do about it.

It is never what is happening that makes us angry.

It is always what we *think* about what's happening.

5. DO THE HEALING FEELINGS EXERCISE. Practice the method described for feeling and releasing the emotional energy.

6. CHANGE YOUR THINKING. Once you've released the emotions, consult your rational mind. Analyze the thoughts behind the emotions. Are they reasonable, true, worth keeping? Will they get you what you want? What thoughts will give you the emotional power to take constructive action?

A situation won't necessarily change just because we change our thinking. But changing our thinking can stimulate the ideas and action necessary to deal with a situation or correct a problem.

7.FORGIVE. Forgiveness unlocks the mind and negative emotional energy. It is a positive means of *giving up*. Give up your sense of entitlement, belief that your way is the right way and the only way, the idea that you cannot be happy unless you get your way. Give up the idea that other people are responsible for your happiness or unhappiness. Give up painful feelings and thoughts of insufficiency, helplessness and anger.

Hatred, anger and resentment have a toxic affect on the body-mind. Attacking another person in anger (physically or mentally) makes us feel guilty, unconsciously if not consciously. No matter how justified we may think we are, we cannot hurt another person without experiencing guilt. That doesn't mean you let people walk all over you! It just means you release the destructive energy of anger so you can deal with things in a calm, rational manner.

Jane hated her ex-husband. Ten years after their divorce, she still blamed him for everything that was wrong in her life. True, he had cheated on her, lied to her, deceived the courts and deprived her of a fair settlement. But to be angry for 10 years? Is anything worth that? It took a while to convince Jane that forgiveness was for her benefit, not his. And that what she needed to forgive was not his actions, but her hatred and the belief that his actions were the cause of her lack of self-esteem, insecurity and unhappiness.

* * * * * *

The fact is that your judgment regarding a particular situation or person may be absolutely right. The object of your anger may be abusing, deceiving, depriving or manipulating you. He/she/it may be absolutely wrong and anger is totally justified. What good does that do you? Anger doesn't solve problems. It makes them worse. But you can transform the energy in anger to positive action. Take responsibility for your well-being, your safety and security. Take positive action to correct wrongs and insure that your needs are met.

Finally, realize that not many people in this world set out to consciously hurt others. Have you ever been annoyed at someone for a perceived slight only to later discover that they hadn't said what you thought? Most of our conflicts are the result of poor communication and misunderstanding. Try to see situations from the other person's point of view. Why are they doing what they're doing? What are their needs? Nothing erases anger faster than compassion.

SUGGESTED READING: *The Anger Trap: Free Yourself from the Frustrations that Sabotage Your Life* by Les Carter

QUOTES TO LIVE BY:

For every minute you are angry you lose sixty seconds of happiness.
— *Ralph Waldo Emerson*

FORGIVENESS
By Geri O'Neill

They speak of reincarnation
And I wonder, if it's so,
Perhaps our paths have crossed before
Not so very long ago.

And did I do unto your soul
What you now do to me?
And are we only working out
A debt to set us free?

Or perhaps you haven't been here
As often yet as I;
Nor had the time to overcome
The faults that I decry.

And even in this present life
I was not at your side
To feel the things that rent your heart
And know what made you cry.

What myriad of thoughts and feelings
Knit the fabric of your being?
Am I to judge you right or wrong
On the little that I'm seeing?

There is much of life ahead,
And I have much to do.
If I would ask forgiveness
I must grant it first to you.

For should I hold my grudges,
And you hold yours for me,
We bind our souls with iron links
Through all eternity.

Chapter 12

STRESS-FULL

...it takes all the running you can do, to keep in the same place.

If you want to get somewhere else, you must run at least twice as fast as that!

Lewis Carroll

We live in a stressed out world. We strive to know and do the right thing, fulfill our role as child, parent, spouse, employer, employee, friend, neighbor. At the same time, we fear we're doing something wrong, not quite good enough. We worry that things will not go the way we want, that we will not get what we need or lose something we value. In one way or another, we feel threatened and inadequate in the face of that threat. We're stressed!

According to the National Institutes of Health, 90% of illness is caused or aggravated by stress. The World Health Organization says job stress is a worldwide epidemic and predicts stress will be the number one killer by 2020.

What exactly is stress? Basically, it's a response to danger. There is a physical and psychological response when we feel endangered in any way.

Whenever we experience a threat to our:

Physical well-being
Identity, self-esteem, self-worth
Beliefs and values
Needs and desires
Expectations.

We react with:

Anxiety
Anger
Fear
Guilt
Grief.

Next, hormones — primarily adrenaline and cortisol — are released and flood the body. That causes immediate changes in the nervous system. Heart rate and blood pressure rise, blood vessels constrict, muscles contract. We go into a state of hyper-alertness, ready to face the threat and fight it out or flee from it. Whether the threat is to the body or our sense of self, the primitive, emotional brain triggers the same physiological response. We become fearful, defensive and aggressive before the rational mind can assess the situation and discern any other way to respond.

Unlike our ancestors, our stress is usually not the result of a life threatening situation. What we feel most often is a threat to our self-image or emotional well-being. But whether we're late for a meeting or being chased by a mountain lion, stress has the same devastating affects. The bottom-line is the same: will I survive this situation intact?

The causes of stress in our modern world are virtually endless. Anything that disrupts the status quo, provokes uncertainty, thwarts our plans, makes us feel we're losing control over ourselves or our lives is stress inducing. Some people face so many stress provoking situations during a day that they end up in a permanent state of stress — constantly on edge, anxious. They don't recover from one alarm before another sounds. Such people are quick to erupt over what appears to others as a trivial matter. They are constantly on the verge of losing self-control. And they're ruining their health. Chronic stress can cause panic attacks and have severe effects on the body and brain.

It's not just threat in the moment we react to. Anticipated problems and difficulties cause a high level of anxiety. Dwelling on an imagined threat or possible problems arouses as much anxiety as if they were real and right in front of us. Even experiences we anticipate with pleasure — a graduation, promotion, marriage, birth of a child — cause stress. The same anxiety is aroused. Can I handle this? How will I handle this? Will it turn out as I desire?

COMMON CAUSES OF STRESS

Major life changes; Isolation/loneliness; Perfectionism; Over-extending/committing Loss of control Worry; Inertia, boredom; Conflict; Unrealistic goals; Illness; Demands of work; Demands of relationships; Sense of lack/need/incompetency; Illness or death of loved ones.

EFFECTS OF STRESS

Physical, emotional and mental tension
Muscle rigidity and pain
Headaches, diarrhea
Weakened immune system; more susceptible to disease
Depression, negativity, irritability, anxiety
Hostile, angry, pessimistic, critical
Fatigue, exhaustion
Restless, inability to concentrate, memory impairment
Hyper-sensitivity

Speeds up aging (Chronic stress shortens life span of cells by 9–17 years)
Lack of appetite or over-eating
Stores fat
Insomnia, digestive problems, personality disorders
Contributes to heart disease, stroke, diabetes, skin conditions.

Chronic stress kills brain cells and destroys nerve cell connections in the brain. Tests on animals proved that hormones released by stress are literally poisonous to the brain's memory centers. A constant current of stress running through the body-mind impairs judgment and performance.

> *Brain cells create ideas. Stress kills brain cells. Stress is not a good idea.*
> — *Frederick Saunders*

Some people are more easily stressed than others. This could be partly due to their genes but is more likely the result of growing up in a threatening environment. People who were exposed to extremely stressful events as children, such as neglect or abuse, tend to be particularly vulnerable to stress as adults. Feelings and fear of being overwhelmed and helpless lie close to the surface for them and are easily triggered.

Stress releases a thrilling rush of adrenalin through the body which can be addictive. Hurrying to finish holiday preparations or working madly to meet a deadline gives a charge of energy that one can come to crave like that morning cup of coffee. Without it, life appears dull. A good crisis puts us on full scale alert, and the super-sensitivity makes us feel vibrant. For this reason, stress addicts are drawn to stressful situations. They need that dose of high drama to feel alive. Unfortunately, the chemicals released by stress are harmful. Sooner or later, stress addicts burn out.

SUGGESTED READING:
Finding Serenity In The Age of Anxiety by Robert Gerzon

QUOTES TO LIVE BY:

> *My life has been filled with terrible misfortunes —*
> *most of which never happened.*
> — *Mark Twain*

LETTING GO OF WORRY

Author Unknown

What if we knew for certain that everything we're worried about today will work out fine?

What if...we had a guarantee that the problem bothering us would be worked out in the most perfect way, and at the best possible time? Furthermore, what if we knew that three years from now we'd be grateful for that problem, and its solution?

What if...we knew that even our worst fear would work out for the best?

What if...we had a guarantee that everything that's happening, and has happened, in our life was meant to be, planned just for us, and in our best interest?

What if...we had a guarantee that the people we love are experiencing exactly what they need in order to become who they're intended to become? Further, what if we had a guarantee that others can be responsible for themselves, and we don't have to control or take responsibility for them?

What if...we knew the future was going to be good, and we would have an abundance of resources and guidance to handle whatever comes our way?

What if...we knew everything was okay, and we didn't have to worry about a thing? What would we do then?

We'd be free to let go and enjoy life.

Chapter 13

STRESS-LESS

Just as anxiety destroys our self-awareness,

so awareness of ourselves can destroy anxiety.

Rollo May

Do this little exercise now…

1. Make tight fists with both your hands. Hold tight, tight, tighter. Notice that you are probably holding your breath too.

2. Let go. Release your hands and your breath.

3. Notice how your hands feel.

You just caused yourself physical tension — stress. Did you shake out your hands when you let go? If not, you put tension in but didn't let it out. Do that now. Shake your hands and wiggle your fingers. Feels better, doesn't it?

If the muscle tension caused by stress is not released, the muscles eventually shorten, become rigid and painful. Pain is a warning signal. It's letting us know that there is imbalance and blockage in the body. Over time, bodies form (actually deform) around these energy blockages. Strength and vitality diminish.

In the course of a normal day, we may frequently tense up and hold our breath for a moment even though we're not having a full blown fight or flight experience. We don't even notice these incidents much less counteract them, but they have a cumulative effect. It's important to be aware of our personal stress provokers and take the time to release those mini-tensions. All that requires is closing your eyes for a minute, taking a deep breath, stretching your muscles.

What consistently causes you stress? Approximately 80% of what people do is in an effort to feel important. If we don't get the recognition we think we deserve — even from strangers — we feel disgruntled. Some people become fretful when they're hungry or if a light isn't left on at night. Notice how you feel the next time you're in the middle of a crowd and people are pushing in, invading your personal space. People have different comfort levels when it comes to space and noise. The faster you release stress, the clearer your body-mind will be.

One reason optimists are healthier than pessimists is because they handle stress better. People who perceive themselves as victims are more vulnerable to stress, depression and disease. The same is true for people who are inflexible and try to change external situations rather than themselves. The only thing we truly have control over is our own thinking.

If you can change it, change it.
If you can't, change yourself.

On some level, we agree to let things upset us. I find a situation stressful because of what I am telling myself: I'm in trouble. Too many demands are being made of me. I can't keep up. I'm losing control. I'm not getting what I want, what I expect, what I need, what makes me happy. Change your thinking and your change your life.

HANDLING STRESS

1. IDENTIFY THE THREAT. The fight or flight reaction serves us well in physically threatening situations. That is rarely the case for most of us. If the threat isn't physical, you can be sure it's to personal identity and security. Probe your anxiety. What part of you feels threatened? Ask yourself questions and be honest in your answers:

> What causes you stress and why?
> What or who consistently sparks anxiety?
> Who are you afraid of?
> What are you afraid of?
> What is in the way of reaching your goals?
> What do you want/need that you're not getting?
> What are you getting that you don't want?
> Who is not meeting your needs, fulfilling your expectations?

2. EXPLORE YOUR FEELINGS. The primitive, emotional brain reacts to threat before the conscious, rational brain even knows what's going on. So, accept the anxiety. Don't fight it. Resistance reinforces it. Feel the feelings. Relax, breathe deeply and let the energy move. It will begin to settle down.

3. CONSULT YOUR RATIONAL MIND. Anxiety and frustration muddle the mind, so don't do anything until emotions subside. When you can think rationally…

TAKE RESPONSIBILITY. What's your part in the problem? How did you contribute to it? Taking responsibility generates power.

BE PRACTICAL. Accept the situation as it is and work with it. Don't waste time and energy wishing things were different. Life is not always going to go the way you want. Be realistic and flexible.

FOCUS ON SOLUTIONS, NOT PROBLEMS. Visualizing the achievement of a goal and not the obstacles is the fastest route to success.

4. WHAT CAN YOU DO? Stress is best dealt with by being faced head on. Deal with problems immediately and address conflicts directly. Look at the situation from different angles. Study, analyze, take it apart, think things through. Let a different interpretation emerge. What good could possibly come of this? What options do you have? Which one would work best?

Don't try to do too much at once. Focus on resolving one issue at a time. Research has proven that multitasking doesn't really work. The brain can switch from one thing to another in less than a second but it can't do two things at once. You'll ease stress, and save time and energy by breaking problems or projects into parts and dealing with each one at a time. Once you make a decision, take action. Indecision is debilitating. Moving forward frees up blocked energy.

When I was writing my first book in the early 80s, I was using a friend's A-frame in the Adirondack Mountains. I was heating solely with wood. As I went through Skip's treasured woodpile day after winter day, it quickly dwindled. I started to worry that he would come by for a visit before another friend of mine arrived with a new load of wood. This may seem like a silly problem to you, but I became obsessed with it. It was a constant nagging worry in the back of my mind. And then it happened. One morning Skip called to say he would be stopping by that afternoon. As soon as I hung up, I called George. "Are you awake?" I asked anxiously when he answered the phone. "I am now," a sleepy voice responded.

When I explained that I was really low on wood and needed it soon, he promised to drop a load off the next day. I would still have to face Skip as he discovered the near empty wood pile, but at least I could promise the situation would be rectified the very next day. As soon as I took that action step, I felt better. My tension eased even though the problem still existed.

As it was, Skip looked at the woodpile as he walked to the front door and simply said, "Getting pretty low on wood, aren't you, Ger?"

Admittedly, I was making a mountain out of a molehill or, in this case, a forest out of a woodpile, but worry does that. It takes seemingly small, insignificant situations and causes tremendous anxiety. Clearly, my stress wasn't about the apparent situation. Running low on wood was not a big deal. What really bothered me was that Skip would think I did not fully appreciate the gift he had given me in the use of the A-frame, or that I didn't value and replace something that was important to him.

Dwelling on a problem magnifies it and increases stress. Soon all our energy goes into worry and tension. We can't think clearly or act productively. **Worry is a substitute for rational thought and positive action.** We need to do something to stop the spiraling stress so we can think logically and act constructively.

LETTING GO

For fast-acting relief, try slowing down.
— *Lily Tomlin*

1. BREATHE. The breath is our life force and first line of defense against stress. Energy moves on the breath. The best and fastest way to ease anxiety and restore equilibrium is slow, deep breathing. Take a moment to close your eyes and inhale. Take the air all the way down into your abdomen. Pause and then exhale fully. Notice the calming effect. Relax your body and your mind will follow.

2. SOUND IT OUT. Sound is the second best way to release energy. Sigh, cry, groan, scream, talk. Talking releases energy and emotion. Express your feelings, thoughts, problems to a trusted confidante who is willing to be a sounding board. Having a caring person just listen eases stress and emotional pain. Talk out loud to yourself if necessary. **Voicing problems aloud activates a different part of the brain and provides greater insight.**

3. WORK IT OUT. Physical activity — exercising, walking, swimming, bike riding — relieves stress. Take a shower or bath. Water is relaxing and healing. Unwind by putting on some music and dancing. **Action counters feelings of helplessness.** Just moving can change your mood. We tend to forget ourselves and problems when totally interested in and actively engaged in an activity.

4. WRITE IT OUT. Write about your problems and feelings. Describing things from the 3rd person perspective restores objectivity. Make a list. The 1,000 things you think you need to do are probably closer to 10. **Writing releases energy, focuses the mind and puts chaotic thoughts in order.**

5. CHANGE YOUR MIND. Reassess the situation. Focus first on what is going right, what's working. Reframe the problem. See it as a challenge, an opportunity. Change your self talk. Saying, "It's okay" over and over eases stress and opens the mind to viewing the situation differently. Tell yourself, "Everything will turn out all right." **See the situation as non-threatening and stress immediately dissolves.**

Stop trying to change the world and change your mind.

6. LET GO. Let things be. Step away from the problem and give it time to unfold. Albert Einstein and Thomas Edison hit many roadblocks in their work. Rather than giving up, they set the problem aside, focused attention elsewhere, and let the solution evolve in its own time and way. Take a mental vacation. Lose yourself in a good movie or book. Take a ride. A change of scenery can spark a different perspective. Allow time and space for things to evolve. **Do what you can, then let go.**

Meditation also relieves tension and stress. We'll be addressing that in the next chapter.

SUGGESTED READING:
Why Zebras Don't Get Ulcers by Robert M. Sapolsky

QUOTES TO LIVE BY:

> *The greatest weapon against stress is our ability*
> *to choose one thought over another.*
> — *William James*

STRESS BUSTERS

1. TAKE A BREAK. Every 1 - 2 hours, take a mini-break from whatever you're doing. Get up. Go for a walk. Have a drink of water.

2. STRETCH. 90% of headaches are caused by tight neck muscles, Stretch your neck, massage your scalp. Gently finger tap your face and scalp.

3. CLEAN UP. Clean out your closets, drawers, desk. Get rid of things you don't use. Clutter provokes a sense of chaos and anxiety.

4. EXERCISE. People who exercise are better able to handle and release stress.

5. NURTURE FRIENDSHIPS. Good friendships are both buffers against and outlets for stress.

6. ONE AT A TIME. Stress comes from trying to handle too much at once and scattering energies. To get the most done in the most efficient manner, concentrate on one thing at a time.

7. TAKE CARE OF YOURSELF. Get enough sleep and eat right.

8. LAUGH, PLAY, CREATE. Laughter releases tension. It increases blood flow to the heart and other organs countering the contraction of blood vessels caused by stress. Humor helps to shift perception, ease anxiety. Playing with children or clay or paints, also relaxes the body and mind, and releases tension.

9. TRUST LIFE. It often has a better solution than what we had in mind. How many times have you said, "It seemed like a disaster at the time but it actually turned out for the best."

Chapter 14

MEDITATION

*A simple yet profound way to
create a healthy body,
a stress-free mind, and a
peaceful sense of well-being.*

Aaron Hoopes

Meditation is not just for attaining spiritual enlightenment. True, it can change brain waves and lead to higher states of consciousness, but there are many other benefits as well. Meditation relaxes the body, calms the emotions and helps the mind work more efficiently. It improves mood, memory, word fluency and reasoning. Meditating regularly affects biological changes in the body and brain which reduce stress, aid sleep, increase energy, endurance, cope-ability and peace of mind.

Most meditative practices involve deep breathing. Some are based on the repetition of sounds. Both are recognized means of lowering blood pressure, easing anxiety, speeding recovery from illness, dealing with depression, fatigue and pain. Full, diaphragmatic breathing has immediate calming affects on the body, nervous system and mind. The increased intake of oxygen and release of carbon dioxide is energizing. Cells are replenished and body chemistry changes. As the body relaxes, so does the brain. Deep breathing improves mental clarity and sharpens awareness.

Sounds great, but isn't it hard? No! All you need to practice meditation is a quiet, comfortable space and a little time. Even the simplest, most basic meditations carry great benefits. Following are directions for several different processes.

1. DEEP BREATHING. Most adults use just their chest muscles when they breathe and don't fill the lungs. Shallow breathing in itself causes anxiety because we're not getting enough oxygen. Abdominal breathing is the healthiest way to breathe. It fills the lungs and sends the most oxygen to the cells, relaxes muscles, improves brain function and, because of the movement of the diaphragm, massages internal organs.

> Find a quiet place where you won't be disturbed.
> Sit or lie down in a comfortable position with spine straight.
> Inhale deeply through your nose. Abdomen inflates, then the chest.
> Slowly exhale through the nose; stomach contracts, diaphragm collapses.
> Exhale fully before inhaling again.
> Repeat for several minutes.
> Keep your full attention on the slow, smooth movement of the breath. Feel it entering and leaving your body.
> Count each inhale and exhale if that helps to stay focused.
> If your mind drifts, simply bring it back to the breath.

Just 3 - 5 minutes of slow, deep breathing twice a day can release stress, reduce muscle and emotional tension, lower blood pressure and heart rate, reduce food cravings and boost energy. For a quick energy lift, make the exhale twice as long as the inhale. For instance, breathe in to a count of three and exhale to a count of six.

The mind remains fixed on a single object... the breath. By practicing this simple yet powerful meditation, one's view of reality changes.
— *S.N. Goenka*

2. RELAXATION & STRESS RELEASE.

Follow the same steps in the previous process.

When you're relaxed and the breath is deep and regular, focus on your feet.

Tighten all the muscles in your feet. Hold for several seconds.

Let go, release the tension. Stretch and wiggle your toes and feet.

As your feet relax, imagine the breath flowing in and our of your feet, your toes, soles, heels, ankles, bones.

Picture the breath as rays of light circulating through the feet, cleansing and renewing the cells, muscles, bones.

Your feet are completely relaxed and rejuvenated.

Gradually move your attention up through every part of your body following the same procedure.

Rest quietly when finished.

Keep breathing deeply and try to remain thought free as you sink into a deep sense of peace.

With 80 - 90% of sensory input coming through vision, just closing the eyes for a moment relaxes brain wave patterns. Throughout the day, close your eyes for a moment and take a few deep breaths to relax.

If you're agitated, try this: Take a deep inhale through the nose. Forcefully exhale all the air through the mouth with the lips pursed. Repeat 5 times. Pause, breathe naturally. Repeat.

3. THE WITNESS STATE. We are more than the learned beliefs and conditioned responses we automatically repeat and identify with. There is always a part of us, sometimes known as the Witness, that is outside what is happening, beyond thoughts and emotions, and not disturbed by them. Dwelling in this state will take you beyond limited self-concepts, increase awareness and peace of mind. In the Witness State, we observe self and life without judgment. Only then can we see and experience things as they really are, undistorted by labels, prejudices and fears. With practice, this heightened awareness can be brought to all our activities.

WITNESSING

Breathe deeply and relax.
Scan your body. Notice how you are sitting, standing, spots of tension, discomfort.
Breathe, relax and watch the tension ease.
Observe your thoughts and feelings. Step apart and watch them. How would you describe them to someone else? Talk about yourself in the 3rd person. Say (your name)_____
is thinking (identify the thought)_____.
Or is feeling _____.
Just notice, don't judge. Don't resist.

Stop at regular intervals throughout the day and observe yourself. What are you doing, feeling, seeing, thinking? Instead of functioning on automatic pilot, be consciously aware of eating, walking, brushing your teeth. Don't judge. Just watch.

If you are able to observe your physical, mental and emotional state, there must be a part of you that is greater than all that. Dwelling in this higher state of mind is enlightening and empowering. We lose it as soon as we become involved in thought, emotion or experience. We say things like, "I am sick," instead of, "My body is experiencing sickness." The sickness has us instead of us having it. It's our whole reality. We become the experience instead of the experiencer.

Much of the time our minds are on automatic pilot and we're unaware of what we're thinking. Try to witness your thoughts for a while. Observe their quality and repetitive nature. Notice how one thought automatically triggers another. Watch your thoughts like a play running across the stage of your mind. Don't resist them. Just watch.

WATCH YOUR THOUGHTS

Picture yourself above and beyond the mental chatter in your brain.

Envision your thoughts as a movie running across your consciousness.

Follow each thought like a wave, forming, cresting and falling.

Don't try to stop or change a thought. Let it run its course.

Observe the flow of one thought into another.

Notice which thoughts have a charge — activate a physical or emotional response.

Notice the thoughts that grab your attention.

When you start to slip into a thought, remind yourself that you're watching a movie, sitting in the audience outside the drama. If something is important, commit to dealing with it when you're finished meditating. Practice this process long enough and your thinking will slow down. Eventually it will cease, for short periods of time at first. Keep at it and periods of mental quiet and deep peace will expand. You'll experience a whole different, higher level of consciousness.

The Witness does just that — witnesses. It doesn't judge or try to change anything. Resistance to a feeling or surrender to it energizes and magnifies it. The feeling takes over and runs you. The Witness is non-reactive. The irony is that in not attempting to control or change things, they often change by themselves. When you step back and watch what a negative thought is doing to you, you're naturally inclined to let it go. By dwelling in the

Witness State, you maintain a sense of peace no matter what is happening.

> A holy man was sitting by the side of the road in India begging for alms. It was cold and a stranger brought him a blanket. The holy man watched the man lay the blanket on his mat and said, "Ah, so."

> A little while later, a thief came by, grabbed the blanket and ran away. "Ah, so," said the holy man. He was watching the drama of life unfold before him without being caught up in or affected by it.

The more you can stay in the Witness State throughout the day, the more you will maintain equilibrium in your life. You will develop self awareness, control over your emotions and conditioned responses. You'll have greater mental clarity and far less stress.

4. SILENCE. If you want to increase self-awareness quickly, spend a *Do Nothing Day*. Absolutely nothing! Don't read, don't talk, don't watch television or listen to music. Don't do anything. Admittedly, this is difficult if you're working or living with someone. Try it for just a few hours. Or half an hour. A sense of anxiety will arise almost immediately. If you're not used to silence and solitude, they can arouse great discomfort. Feel it. Don't resist. Don't run away. Breathe through it.

After the initial resistance, the body and mind start to settle down. Thoughts drift away. Senses become sharper. At this point, a feeling of emptiness often surfaces. Sink into it. It will pass and you'll sink deeper, into a state of utter peace. Simply be in the silent space. Among the many gifts to be found there are greater awareness, insight, pure emotion and clear perception.

> *Silence is the mother of truth.*
> — *Benjamin Disraeli*

Meditation is refreshing and restorative to body, mind and mood. It increases inner peace and builds coping skills. Regular practice will enable you to achieve a relaxed, peaceful state of mind quickly. If you're not interested in the higher consciousness aspects of meditation, use deep breathing to release stress and re-energize yourself through the day. Consciously deepen and slow the breath to stop anger and anxiety, restore calm and rational thinking. Think of it as quiet time. Whether you take a walk, go swimming, play a musical instrument, paint or read a book, give yourself time for relaxation and restoration, self-reflection and awareness.

SUGGESTED READING:

The Attention Revolution - Unlocking the Power of the Focused Mind by B. Alan Wallace, Ph.D.

QUOTES TO LIVE BY:

...there is an intense delight in abandoning faulty states of mind and in cultivating helpful ones in meditation.

— *Dalai Lama*

Chapter 15

THE X WORD

I have to exercise in the morning before my brain figures out what I'm doing.

Marsha Doble

Does the X word—exercise—raise resistance in you? Hopefully, this chapter will change your mind, and make exercise something you want to do every day. Just wait till you learn how important it is to body, brain and emotions, how good it can make you feel, how critical it is to health and well-being.

Exercise is important at every age and absolutely essential to aging well. According to the International Council of Active Aging, only about one in four people over age 50 exercise. A mere 16% of people over 65 exercise for at least 30 minutes a day. Fortunately, no matter when we start, following a daily exercise program produces immediate results. Doctors have noted dramatic improvements in flexibility and mobility in patients who embark on an exercise program — even those who started in their 90s.

"The human body is extremely resilient," says aging expert Jessie Jones. "It will respond to the demands you place on it, no matter what your age." And sports medicine specialist Dr. Ralph Brovard says, "Daily exercise is perhaps the most powerful tool you can prescribe for yourself; a variety of regular activity helps prevent cardiovascular disease, type 2 diabetes, osteoporosis, arthritis and just about every other affliction that strikes us as we age."

Exercise will improve the shape you're in no matter what shape you're in or when you start. Many gyms have classes for seniors and trainers to guide them, but consult a doctor before beginning.

EXERCISE and YOUR BODY

EXERCISE improves balance, flexibility, mobility, endurance, strength, stamina, strengthens lungs, boosts immune system, aids sleep, raises energy levels, reduces stress and risk of diabetes, increases muscle mass, helps burn calories, improves oxygen intake, reduces inflammation, obesity and the risk of depression, osteoarthritis, some kinds of cancer, broken bones and dying prematurely.

EXERCISE and YOUR HEART

EXERCISE dramatically cuts the risk of heart disease and stroke. It increases circulation, cleans arteries, builds blood vessels, lowers blood pressure and strengthens the heart. It can prevent and even reverse some heart damage.

Lack of exercise causes heart muscles to stiffen which can be a precursor to heart failure. Dramatic improvements in heart function and flexibility have been documented in elderly, sedentary people who maintained a physical training program for a year or more. A study from the University of Texas Southwestern Medical Center in Dallas on men in their early 50s discovered that six months of modest exercise (about 4 and 1/2 hours a week) brought their cardiovascular capacity back to the levels it was at in their 20s. In effect, six months of training reversed 30 years of aging!

While exercise can reduce the risk of heart disease, it is also important to acknowledge and treat psycho-social factors. Depression, stress, mental and emotional problems are contributory factors to coronary disease.

EXERCISE and YOUR BRAIN

EXERCISE virtually cleanses the brain, flushing away the plaque build up believed to cause Alzheimer's Disease. It can stimulate neurogenesis, the birth of new cells, in certain areas of the brain. Exercise increases blood flow in the brain, heightens mental acuity, improves alertness, awareness, cognitive abilities of learning, memory, planning, scheduling, task coordination and attention, has positive biochemical effects and protects the brain from damage, disease and aging.

Your brain accounts for 2% of your body weight but uses 20% of the oxygen you breathe. To keep oxygen rich blood flowing to the brain, it, needs aerobic exercise. Adults who exercise have more grey matter representing more brain cells. They recover faster from strokes or brain injury. Daily exercise can give a 30% boost to brain power and cut the risk of Alzheimer's Disease and Parkinson's. The director of the Alzheimer Disease Center at a Chicago Medical Center explained, "Exercise releases chemicals that protect brain cells and keep them performing at top speed."

Exercise is a proven anti-dote to depression. It activates the same systems in the brain as anti-depressant drugs and has similar effects without negative side effects. Stretching and flexibility exercises performed 15 to 20 minutes three days a week resulted in a 29% decline in depressive symptoms among participants. Exercise releases endorphins which elevate mood, improve reaction time and cognitive function, enhance self-concept and counter stress.

For all this, surely we can find a little time each day to exercise. Ideally, you should alternate aerobics and muscle building, but housework, gardening, dancing, biking, walking, golf and stretching can all be considered forms of moderate exercise. You'll soon see improvements in your health, endurance, strength, balance, flexibility, appearance, energy, attitude and mental acuity. No matter when you start! So, now that I hope I've convinced you that you MUST exercise for health and longevity, these are some questions we need to ask…

HOW MUCH?

The upside is that it doesn't take a huge amount of time to maintain a decent fitness level: 90 minutes of aerobic activity and 60 minutes of weight training WEEKLY will do it. Just 20 minutes of weight lifting a few times a week helped people regain strength and independence. At the very least, try to exercise 20 - 30 minutes a day. The more time devoted to it, however, the greater the rewards.

Listen to your body. Don't overdo it. Older bodies take longer to recover so rest during and after workouts. Increase your activity level gradually. Go a little faster or longer as your strength builds. When it comes to lifting weights, slow with accurate form is far more beneficial than many, speedy repetitions.

WHAT KIND?

Whatever you do, do something! Start by incorporating physical activities you enjoy into your life on a regular basis. At least one should be aerobic. As you start to feel more fit and energized, add muscle building to your routine. If you are just embarking upon an exercise program, be sure to choose something pleasurable so you'll keep at it. Beginning classes in yoga, Pilates and tai chi are enjoyable and great for easing into shape. They improve posture and flexibility as well as strength.

There are many different types and levels of yoga. If you are new to the practice, look for a beginner's class that includes stretching, breathing and meditation. Yoga is wonderful for maintaining balance and flexibly. It also provides an internal workout which improves circulation and gently massages the organs. Pilates improves alignment, posture and coordination through exercises that combine breath control with strengthening the core of the body. It's especially good for abdominal and pelvic muscles, the lower back and buttocks.

Tai chi programs designed specifically for seniors have had great success in improving strength, endurance, concentration and balance. Even people with arthritis or physical pains and disabilities are usually able to follow the slow, graceful movements. tai chi is a proven stress reducer and has been successful in lowering blood pressure, relieving pain, improving heart function and enhancing the immune system. Tests have shown that it also helps combat insomnia. Emory University School of Medicine did a study of 200 people age 70 and over. A 15-week tai chi class reduced the risk of multiple falls in participants by over 47%.

We become less flexible as we age because the connective tissue in the body deteriorates. There are classes that concentrate only on stretching. Once you know the proper technique, it is easily done on your own. Daily stretching keeps joints mobile and releases muscle tension. It improves posture, balance and increases range of motion.

Without resistance exercise (strength training) we lose 6 pounds of muscle a decade. That lowers metabolism and makes us more susceptible to disease. We also lose muscle rapidly if we're sick, injured or immobile for two weeks or more. The good news is that it only takes 20 minutes a day 2 - 3 times a week for 10 - 12 weeks to rebuild 3 pounds of muscle and increase metabolism by 7%. At the same time you'll be reducing blood pressure, increasing bone mass and improving gastrointestinal efficiency. Building muscles reduces frailty and the risk of falling.

EXERCISE TIPS

Get proper training. Warm up before, cool down after. Drink water before, during and after.

Visualize improvement. Visualizing exercises reinforces the associated neural patterns and can improve performance. Visualization can help build weak muscles, but you need to do it for at least 20 minutes a day to produce notable results. That's meant to be an adjunct to physical exercise, not a replacement!

Practice balance. More than one third of people over 65 and half of people over 75 have balance problems. Practice maintaining your balance while standing on one foot. Have a support close at hand to steady yourself. Also, when you get out of bed or stand up, get in the habit of placing both feet flat on the floor and waiting a few seconds so you don't get dizzy. Stand up slowly and center your weight over your feet before walking.

Mix it up. Vary your program; challenge yourself with change. Aside from the basics of walking, stretching, aerobic and resistance training, add some different, enjoyable exercises like biking, swimming, gardening. All physical activity is good. The more vigorous, the better.

SUGGESTED READING: *Staying Strong: A Senior's Guide to a More Active and Independent Life* by Lorie A. Schleck

Fitness for Seniors: Amazing Body Breakthroughs for Super Health by Frank K. Wood

MORE INFORMATION: www.aarpfitness.com/24; www.realage.com; www.healthandage.com

QUOTES TO LIVE BY:

> *Movement is a medicine for creating change in a person's physical, emotional, and mental states.*
> — *Carol Welch*

SIMPLE STRETCHES

Take a stretch to the point of tension and hold for 20 - 30 seconds. Don't bounce. Keep breathing. If tension eases, stretch a little farther.

1. WARM UP:

Shake your arms and hands. Wiggle your fingers.
Roll your wrists in circles, clockwise and counterclockwise.
Hold onto back of chair and shake your feet and legs.
Rotate ankles in both directions. Stretch foot forward, pull back.
Hands on hips, knees gently bent, roll hips in a circle one way 8 times, and then the other.

2. HEAD and NECK:

Look over your right shoulder. Use right hand to gently push your chin a little further and hold. Same on opposite side.
Push your chin to your chest and then stretch your head all the way back. Repeat 10 times.
Put chin to chest, intertwine fingers behind your head. Try to raise head against resistance from your hands.

3. SHOULDERS:

Intertwine your fingers, roll your shoulders forward and stretch your arms out in front of you with palms facing outward. Slowly raise arms overhead.
Put your arms behind your back, clasp hands together and stretch out your arms as straight as possible while bending forward.

Raise your shoulders to your ears and drop. Repeat 10 times.
Roll your shoulders forward and backward. 10 times each.

4. ADDITIONAL STRETCHES:

Arms overhead, stretch to each side. Twist side to side as far as you can. Let arms swing free.

Grab left hip with right hand, twist to left, hold. Change sides.

Raise one foot behind you and pull the ankle toward your buttocks.

Roll forward and hang loosely. Try to touch toes.

Raise arms out to side. Make big and little circles.

Chapter 16

TAKE A WALK

I have two doctors, my left leg and my right.

G.M. Trevelvan

One form of exercise practically everyone can do every day is walk. As human beings we're built to move, we need to move. For good health and longer life, we should walk a minimum of 30 minutes a day. If necessary, that can be broken into 2 or even 3 segments. So, no excuses. Let's get walking.

Walking is good for what ails you. High intensity walking resulted in the most health benefits for older people according to a Japanese study. Another study found that a daily walk increased survival rates of heart attack victims by 80%. Walking involves hundreds of muscles and the rhythmic movement massages internal organs, improves circulation and increases peristalsis which influences digestion, assimilation and elimination.

WALKING strengthens leg muscles, reduces frailty and risk of falling, increases metabolism, mental and physical energy, oxygen intake, raises heart rate, lowers risk of heart attack, osteoporosis, stroke, diabetes, some cancers, reduces stress, builds muscle, improves sleep and outlook, helps to lose weight and maintain weight loss.

All forms of exercise including leisurely walking can reduce the risk of dementia. A Harvard Public Health School study of nearly 20,000 older women found that those who exercised 2 - 3 hours a week did much better on tests of memory and cognitive function than inactive women. The more physically active, the better they did, but just walking at an easy pace produced positive results. Similar tests performed on men reached the same conclusion.

Then there are the psychological benefits of a daily walk. It can be a chance to spend quality time with a partner or friend, quiet time for reflection, an opportunity to get fresh air and your Vitamin D dosage from the sun. Synchronize your breathing with walking and it becomes a form of meditation.

Angels whisper to a man when he goes for a walk.
— *Raymond Inmon*

If physical disability or imbalance make walking difficult, riding a stationary bike provides many of the same health benefits. One 6 month study of 22 people over 80 years of age showed that both riding a stationary bike and walking on a treadmill twice a week for about 20 minutes resulted in significant improvements in stamina, oxygen levels and blood pressure.

For most people, walking is the ideal exercise. You can do it any time any place. All that's needed is a good pair of shoes. We should be walking 10,000 steps a day and 12,000 to lose weight. All walking is good for you, but the more you push, the more you gain. To make walking aerobic, gradually increase distance, incline and speed.

HOW TO WALK

Start at a slow, easy pace.
Head up, back straight, arms relaxed.
Lift shoulders up, back and down.
Knees flexed.
Breathe deeply.
Gradually increase speed.
Attain a steady pace with a good stride.
Bend your arms at 90 degree angles. Pump them back to your rear end and forward to mid-chest.
The faster you move your arms, the faster your feet will move.
Be aware of the movement of your body and develop a sense of rhythm, grace and flow.

If you are not used to walking and find it strenuous, start with a leisurely ten minute walk. Work up to thirty minutes a day and commit to maintaining that. Outside, inside, on a treadmill, wherever. As stamina increases, walk faster and/or farther to see greater results. If walking is your primary exercise, walk fast enough to raise your heart rate. After a certain age, weight goes on faster and comes off slower. Want to counteract that? Take an extra 2,000 steps a day. Add a 10 minute after dinner walk and you'll increase metabolism and aid digestion while walking those extra steps.

SUGGESTED READING: *Walking: The Five Mindful Steps for Lifelong Health and Energy* by Danny Dreyer and Katherine Dreyer

MORE INFORMATION: www.walking.about.com

QUOTES TO LIVE BY:

Above all, do not lose your desire to walk.. Every day
I walk myself into a state of well-being and walk away from every illness.
I have walked myself into my best thoughts, and I know of no thought so
burdensome that one cannot walk away from it.

— Soren Kierkegaard

Chapter 17

FOOD FOR THOUGHT

DID YOU KNOW...

Tell me what you eat, I'll tell you who you are.

Anthelme Brillat-Savarin

An additional 10 pounds of body weight feels like 30 pounds to your knees when you're walking?

The ideal blood pressure is 115/76?

Any movement including fidgeting increases metabolism?

Your metabolic rate drops by 40% if you starve yourself for more than 12 hours? The body starts storing fat.

Obesity has been linked to declines in memory and attention span in 30 year olds as well as older people?

Diet, like exercise, is of crucial importance to physical, mental and emotional health. Eating natural foods, lots of fruits and vegetables, and eliminating bad fats and sugars can significantly cut the risk of heart disease, diabetes, Alzheimer's, and a host of other ailments. But in spite of the many books, programs, products and billions of dollars spent on nutrition and weight loss, obesity and related diseases are on the rise around the world.

According to one study, approximately 7% of the global population is obese, and 1.6 billion people fall into the obese or overweight category. In the United States, the obesity number is a shocking 30%. American women ate approximately 300 more calories and men about 170 more calories per day in 2000 than they did in 1971. That accounts for the fact that 65% of Americans are overweight, up from 46% in 1980, and expected to rise to 75% by 2015. Americans rank 9th on the world's fattest countries list. New Zealand is 17th.

One in three Americans has diabetes or pre-diabetes. As developing nations adopt high fat Western eating habits, the incidence of obesity, diabetes and heart disease is rising across the globe. The World Health Organization believes obesity to be the biggest unrecognized health problem in the world.

In spite of our best dieting efforts, Americans on average are gaining 1 to 2 pounds a year. The problem is what we're consuming. 90% of our food dollars go to processed foods. The sugar in sodas is the number one source of calories. Psychological factors related to what and when we eat should also be taken into consideration when fighting the battle of the bulge.

WHAT'S EATING YOU?

Our emotions at any given time influence what we feel like eating. When we're down, we want comfort food like pasta dishes. Feeling lonely or empty? Anything that buries those feelings and fills you up. When we feel mistreated or hurt, we like to soothe ourselves with treats — sweets and ice cream. Anxious or highly stressed people tend to want foods that keep them chewing.

A lot of these feelings come in combinations and can lead to a feeding frenzy. But food doesn't heal emotions. They come back bigger and stronger the next time. That's why it is important to stop, acknowledge what you're feeling, accept it and work with it.

Next time, you have a craving, do the Healing Feelings exercise described earlier. Allow the feelings behind the hunger to surface and be felt. Take action to correct the causes for your emotional disturbance. But even with those positive steps, you will be fighting a losing battle if you don't wean yourself off sugar, starchy white carbohydrates and bad fats.

A healthy body naturally desires what's good for it. Once we've flooded our systems with unnatural foods, we develop different tastes and disastrous cravings. Sugar is addictive. Except for natural sugar found in honey and fruit, most people are allergic and hyper-sensitive to white sugar.

SUGAR ISN'T TOO SWEET

In 1700, the average person consumed 7½ pounds of sugar a year. Today, consumption is 150 pounds. Too much sugar has a poisonous effect on the body and brain. It contributes to emotional instability, depression, hyperactivity and aggression. It can affect learning and thinking, speed aging and increase the risk of Alzheimer's Disease. Sugar has negative effects on the immune system, eyesight, teeth and gums. It can cause headaches, arthritis, atherosclerosis and heart disease. It contributes to osteoporosis and cancer. Too much sugar is almost as aging to your skin as smoking and over exposure to sun. Sugar by any other name — corn syrup, fructose, dextrose — is just as toxic to your system.

GOOD FAT/BAD FAT

A three-year-old said this of her Christmas dinner:
"I don't like the turkey, but I like the bread he ate."
— Author Unknown

Americans are carrying about 5 billion pounds of excess fat, and the fat around the belly is the most dangerous. The ideal waist size is 32 inches or less for a woman and 35 inches for a man. Saturated fat, chronic stress and lack of exercise are the fat culprits.

Fear of fat has made people shy away from all fats and buy artificial low fat foods. But there are good fats we absolutely need like those found in fish, avocados and nuts. Low fat artificial foods are partially responsible for the rise in weight gain. Rather than satisfy, they stimulate ongoing hunger as does low blood sugar.

Bad fats increase the inflammatory response which makes one prone to obesity. Bad fats are those that are solid at room temperature. Good fats are liquid at room temperature. The best oils are extra virgin olive oil or cold press canola oil.

Are you getting enough omega-3 fatty acids? Most people aren't. Symptoms of a deficiency are dry skin, fatigue, joint pain, depression, poor concentration. Omega-3 fatty acids reduce inflammation, cholesterol, risk of heart disease, obesity, cancer, Alzheimer's Disease and other dementias.

There is evidence that Alzheimer's Disease starts 10 - 15 years before it is apparent, and it's influenced by what we eat. The high blood pressure and cholesterol that accompany extra pounds have a deleterious affect on the brain as well as the heart. The toxins in processed foods cause inflammation which is at the root of most if not all disease. Alzheimer's Disease is highest in countries with high consumption of bad fats: United States, United Kingdom, Canada, Mexico, Spain, Italy, Finland, Sweden. China, Nigeria, Japan, Singapore have the lowest incidences of Alzheimer's.

GOOD FATS		BAD FATS	
Salmon	Herring	Butter	Margarine
Sardines	Tuna	Bacon, lamb, steak	Whole milk
Free range		Donuts	Ice cream
chicken	Avocado	Fried food	Processed food
Nuts	Flax seed		

EATING FOR HEALTH

Did you ever stop to taste a carrot? Not just eat it, but taste it?
You can't taste the beauty and energy of the earth in a Twinkie.
— *Astrid Alauda*

A healthy diet provides nutrients necessary for optimal body and brain performance. Cold water fish is good brain food. Foods high in anti-oxidants protect the brain and keep it sharp. A balanced diet of good carbohydrates, fats and protein in every meal helps to attain and maintain a healthy weight. It also slows the aging process. Fruits and vegetables lower blood pressure and cut the risk of heart disease by 21%. One clove a day of garlic cuts it by 25%. Here are some tips for developing a healthy diet...

EAT

Small, healthy meals or snacks every 2 - 3 hours.
9 servings of fruit and vegetables daily. (1 serving = 1 handful)
A colorful variety of fruits and vegetables.
Skin free poultry.
1 ounce of nuts a day. (Especially walnuts)
Fish high in omega fatty acids 3 times a week.
Fiber and whole grains.
Healthy snacks: Fruit, cut up vegetables, nuts, seeds, whole grain cereal or bread

Most people don't get all the anti-oxidants, vitamins and minerals they need from food. A good multi-vitamin is not always enough. Many older people are deficient in anti-oxidants, coQ10, Vitamin B12, high B complex vitamins, vitamin D and calcium. Folic acid is believed to reduce the risk of Alzheimer's disease. Consult your doctor or a nutritionist for supplements you may need.

ELIMINATE

Processed foods
Trans fasts, saturated fats and products with hydrogenated on the label
Fatty red meats
White pasta, rice, bread, refined flour
Sugar, high fructose, corn syrup.

TO LOSE WEIGHT

In general, mankind, since the improvement in cookery,
eats twice as much as nature requires.
— *Benjamin Franklin*

Bodies adapt to weight gain and resist losing it. Be patient. You have to re-educate your body. It's worth the effort. Burning off those extra pounds will increase energy levels as well as health. Aside from eliminating what's been mentioned, here are some hints to help shed pounds…

1. Drink a couple of glasses when hungry and before meals to help fill you up and decrease appetite.

2. Start meals with soup or salad low in calories to squelch appetite.

3. Fiber is filling and kills cravings.

4. Eat often so you don't get hungry and binge on the wrong foods.

5. Smaller plates and portions. The bigger the plate, the more you're likely to put on it. If you're eating every $2 - 3$ hours, it shouldn't be difficult to cut portion sizes.

6. Take your time. Look at and smell your food. Eat slowly and chew well. The message that we're full doesn't reach the brain for about 20 minutes. If we eat fast or order dessert immediately after dinner, that message doesn't register and we're likely to overeat. Put down utensils between bites.

7. Apples, berries, non-tropical fruits and celery are good fat fighters. They limit the amount of fat that cells can absorb.

8. Build muscle to burn calories. Muscle raises metabolism and burns about 50 calories a day per pound. A pound of fat only burns 1 – 3 calories.

9. If you are a soda drinker, stop or cut back.

10. Stop eating when 80% full.

12. Keep healthy snacks on hand.

13. Exercise. To burn the most fat, exercise for at least 40 minutes or walk 3 miles at a leisurely pace. After dinner, take a short walk.

14. Exercise. As little as 5 minutes of exercise at key times during the day can increase your calorie burning power. Those times are within an hour of getting out of bed, within ½ hour of eating and in the early evening.

15. Get rid of stress! Stress produces insulin and cortisol which causes the body to store fat.

If you start losing weight without trying to, it could be a sign of a health problem. See your doctor.

SUGGESTED READING: Any or all of Jean Carper's books.
Super Foods Health Style: Proven Strategies for Lifelong Health
by Steven G. Pratt, M.D. and Kathy Matthews

Newsletters*: Julian Whitaker, M.D. *Health and Healing: Your Definitive Guide To Alternative Health and Anti-Aging Medicine.*

Stephen Sinatra, M.D. *The Sinatra Health Report: An Insider's Guide To Smart Medicine and Longevity.*

*Charge a fee

MORE INFORMATION: www.nutritiondata.com;
www.sparkpeople.com; www.jeancarper.com

QUOTES TO LIVE BY:

> *If you are ever at a loss to support a flagging conversation,*
> *introduce the subject of eating.*
> — *Leigh Hunt*

Chapter 18

THE MIRACLE WORKERS

If I'd known I was going to live so long,
I'd have taken better care of myself.
Leon Eldred

How much do you think genes are responsible for how we age? Only 30%! Tests done on identical twins with opposite lifestyles revealed dramatic differences in aging. Researchers concluded that dementia is often the result of an unhealthy lifestyle lacking in physical and mental activity. Aside from exercise and diet, there are several other things essential to total well-being, raising energy levels and maintaining a good weight.

WATER

I believe that water is the only drink for a wise man.
— Henry David Thoreau

We can't live very long without water. It is of vital importance to every cell, organ and function of the body. Human beings are actually walking bodies of water. Blood is 83% water, muscles 75%, brains 74%, bones 22%.

FACTS ABOUT WATER

Necessary to maintain muscle tone
Helps prevent sagging skin
Helps rid the body of waste
Helps relieve constipation
Improves endocrine function
Improves mental performance
Natural appetite suppressant
Regulates body temperature
Regulates metabolism.

A drop of just 2% in hydration can reduce energy levels by 20 % and affect the ability to concentrate.

SYMPTOMS and EFFECTS OF DEHYDRATION

Physical and mental sluggishness
Short term memory impairment
Feelings of anxiety, confusion, irritability, apathy
Headache, dizziness, fatigue
Dry mouth, dry skin
Constipation
Dark urine
Fluid retention
Weight gain
Reduction in blood volume
Cramps, chills, nausea or vomiting
Increase in heart rate
Drop in blood pressure
Production of cholesterol.

Dehydration means there is not enough water in the cells. The body experiences this as a threat to survival. It starts retaining fluids. Water retention results in weight gain, swollen feet, ankles, legs and hands. Kidney function is affected and skin dries out.

"When dehydrated, the body preserves the water supply to critical organs, such as the brain and the heart, but 'cuts off water' to peripheral organs such as skin," explains German Todorov, PhD, biomedical researcher.

The body retains water because it needs water. Therefore, the best treatment for water retention is to drink more water. Water is a natural diuretic. The standard recommendation is at least eight 8 ounce glasses of water a day. A better way to gauge how much water you need is to drink at least one quart of filtered water for every 50 pounds of body weight. If you live in a very hot climate or exercise and sweat a lot, you need to drink more. If you drink a lot of diuretic beverages (sodas, coffee, tea), you need to drink more.

WATER and WEIGHT

The body's need for water is sometimes mistaken as hunger. Before grabbing something to eat, drink a glass of water. If you're still hungry, it won't take as much to fill you up. Drinking enough water every day is essential for metabolizing fat and losing weight. If you're overweight, you need more water than the average person to flush the excess waste and fat out of your system.

SUNSHINE

The sun is nature's Prozac.
— *Astrid Alauda*

Oh, the bad reputation sunshine has acquired. But we couldn't live without it. Of course, anything taken to extremes can be dangerous. But that means too little sunshine is also bad. Fear of getting skin cancer from the sun has led to a sharp rise in Vitamin D deficiency, and a host of related physical problems.

Dr. Bess Dawson-Hughes, director of the Bone Metabolism Laboratory at Tufts University says, "We absolutely have a huge problem with vitamin D deficiency." It affects millions in the United States and over a billion people worldwide. The problem is especially common in older adults. The number of nursing home residents with D deficiency may be as high as 80%.

Humans need sunlight. It has nutrients we can't get any other way. The body makes Vitamin D when sun touches skin. It is nearly impossible to get adequate amounts of vitamin D from diet. **Sunlight is the absolutely best way to get Vitamin D.** We'd have to drink at least 10 glasses of fortified milk to get the necessary minimum. And we could get the same amount from just a few minutes of sunlight. Lack of Vitamin D leads to many physical and mental problems.

VITAMIN D DEFICIENCY is linked to…

Osteoporosis (50 – 70% of people who suffer hip fractures are deficient in Vitamin D)
Rickets
Multiple sclerosis
Diabetes
16 types of cancer
Muscle weakness and pain
Neurological disorders
Decreased cognitive function
Fibromyalgia
Rheumatoid arthritis
Type 1 diabetes
Depression.

Extreme Vitamin D deficiency may cause chronic pain. Swiss researchers reported that unexplained pain "disappeared" within one to three months after treating patients with vitamin D.

Dr. Michael Holick, author of "The UV Advantage," told Mike Adams of Natural News.com: Sufficient levels of vitamin D are crucial for the absorption of calcium in the intestines. Without sufficient vitamin D, your body cannot absorb calcium, rendering calcium supplements useless. Chronic Vitamin D deficiency cannot be reversed overnight: it takes months of vitamin D supplementation and sunlight exposure to rebuild the body's bones and nervous system.

Vitamin D affects the entire body. An Australian study of 1,500 elderly women found that the higher the levels of vitamin D, the less likely they were to fall and break bones. Sun also stimulates the thyroid gland and increases serotonin which makes us feel good. A University of Pittsburgh study found that patients on the sunny side of the hospital recovered faster from spinal surgery than those on the dimmer side. They also needed less painkillers per hour.

VITAMIN D

Helps body absorb calcium and build stronger bones
Strengthens immune system
Helps fight disease
Reduces inflammation
Helps prevent heart disease
Helps prevent cancer
Helps prevent high blood pressure
May slow aging.

HOW MUCH?

Many experts agree that a minimum of 1,000 international units a day is necessary. That can be had from moderate sun exposure, the only reliable way to generate vitamin D in your body. According to Dr. Dawson-Hughes, 10 minutes a day of unprotected sun exposure is sufficient to produce the vitamin D we need. But it really depends on the pigmentation of your skin and how far you live from the equator. Protect yourself from over exposure and sunburn.

SLEEP

Sleep is the golden chain that ties health and our bodies together.
— Thomas Dekker

Bodies and brains need rest. We would die sooner from sleep deprivation than starvation. Sleeping well and long enough is crucial to health. Lack of sleep affects the ability to concentrate, learn and remember. Coordination and judgment are impaired when we're overtired. We're more likely to make bad choices like eating the wrong foods.

SLEEP DEPRIVATION

Weakens immune system
Affects metabolism and hormonal balance
Increases susceptibility to infection, high blood pressure, weight gain
Can hasten aging and the onset of diabetes
Increases risk of heart attack
Disrupts serotonin levels
Causes irritability, impatience and depression
Decreases brain activity
Good sleepers have less illness, healthier appearance and live longer.

SLEEP

Releases and counters stress
Improves mood, concentration
Increases energy
Builds and maintains brain cell connections
Restores and rejuvenates the body

Necessary for processing information
Essential to learning and memory.

During sleep, we are doing mental housecleaning. The brain is filtering through memories, determining what is worth keeping and what can be discarded. It consolidates what we've learned and strengthens the skills we've used. Going to sleep after learning something new helps the brain absorb and retain the information.

HOW MUCH?

Studies show that the optimal amount of high quality sleep is 7 – 8 hours a night for men and 6½ - 7 hours for women. Most children need 9 –10 hours per night. Less affects academic performance.

It usually takes about 10 minutes to fall asleep and 2½ hours of uninterrupted sleep before it becomes restorative. The longer you sleep without interruption, the better. That's when rapid eye movement and slow-wave sleep patterns occur and do restorative work. Snoring and falling asleep as soon as your head hits the pillow could be signs of sleep deprivation.

As people age, they often sleep less soundly. Sleep patterns change. Insomnia is not uncommon. Catnaps can help. A study by NASA found that alertness rose 54 % and performance 34 % after a 25 minute nap. Be careful; sleeping more than an hour during the day may hinder falling asleep at night.

* * * * * *

If there's a sudden decline in your physical or mental state, it is most likely not due to aging. It could be caused by a poor diet or the medication you're taking. Or it could be the result of dehydration, sun or sleep deprivation.

SUGGESTED READING:
Dr. Mercola's Total Health Program by Joseph Mercola, Brian Vaszily, Kendra Pearsall and Nancy Lee Bentley

MORE INFORMATION: www.prevention.com; www.naturalnews.com; www.sleepfoundation.org

QUOTES TO LIVE BY:

> *The best six doctors anywhere*
> *And no one can deny it*
> *Are sunshine, water, rest, and air*
> *Exercise and diet.*

Nursery rhyme quoted by Wayne Fields, What the River Knows

SLEEP AIDS

1. For several hours before bed, AVOID: sugars, caffeine, alcohol, liquids, strenuous exercise, stimulating television shows or reading material. People are 7 times more likely to have heartburn if they go to bed within 3 hours of eating. Drinking fluids increases likelihood of waking up to go to the bathroom. Sugar and caffeine can keep you awake. Alcohol may put you to sleep, but it suppresses REM won't be a refreshing, restorative sleep.

2. To help you sleep: a warm bath, cool room, glass of milk, instant oatmeal with banana.

3. Have a consistent sleep schedule so your internal clock adapts.

4. If possible, don't use an alarm clock to wake up.

5. Easy stretches, deep breathing and progressive relaxation can help you fall asleep faster and sleep better.

6. Sleep in a very dark room and don't turn on a bright light if you awaken during the night. Bright lights tell the body to wake up and it stops producing melatonin.

7. Calm down, unwind. Take a short leisurely walk. Read inspirational material. Listen to soft, relaxing music.

8. If you get cold feet, wear socks.

9. Try to get to bed by 11 pm.

10. Insomnia can be caused by vitamin deficiencies. Make sure you are getting enough Vitamin B6 and B12, calcium and magnesium. Melatonin levels decrease with age, so taking melatonin aids sleep and cellular rejuvenation. Also, check your medications. Many have negative effects on sleep.

Chapter 19

YOUR AMAZING BRAIN

DID YOU KNOW...

If I had to live my life again I would have made a rule to read some poetry and listen to some music at least once a week; for perhaps the parts of my brain now atrophied could thus have been kept active through use.

Charles Darwin

About 95% of what science now knows about the brain has been discovered in the last 20 years.

Brains are malleable, constantly reconfiguring. They change shape and chemistry with every experience, thought and emotion.

The average adult human brain weighs only 3 pounds but uses 20% of the body's oxygen.

30% of the water you consume is used by your brain.

40% of the nutrients you consume are used by the brain.

There are one hundred billion nerve cells in your brain and more connections between brain cells than there are stars in the universe!

Your brain is a living and vital organ responsible for consciousness, intelligence and emotions. It cannot store water and nutrients so it needs constant nourishment in the form of oxygen, glucose, fluids, exercise and mental activity. The more oxygen the brain gets, the better it functions. That's why exercising both body and brain are of crucial importance. We don't want to be like the man who went to apply for Social Security and was told: "I'm sorry, sir, feeling 65 isn't enough. You have to be 65."

Nowhere is the saying "Use it or Lose" more true than when spoken of the brain. Every time your brain is stimulated, it either reinforces a neural circuit or grows dendrites — connections between brain cells. And it is these connections that assure mental acuity, not the number of brain cells you have.

DENDRITES

The word dendrite comes from a Greek word meaning tree. Dendrites are branch like protrusions that grow off brain cells. Every neuron is covered with 10,000 - 100,000 dendrites. And the branches have branches. They're called spines, and can number from 100,000 to 1 million.

Dendrites reach out and interconnect brain cells forming an intricate web. There is a continuous exchange of information between all the cells in the body; thousands of neurons are involved in even the simplest of actions. Dendrites are the Information Highway of the brain, sending and receiving signals that travel through the brain and body electro-chemically. If dendrites atrophy from lack of use, it is difficult for the brain to receive and retrieve information. The brain's communication network breaks down. Dementia is associated with the loss or shortening of dendrites.

The exciting news is that barring some diseases, we can build new dendrites at any age. The more inter-neural connections, the better the brain functions. The number of new connections a human being can make in a lifetime is 1 followed by 6.2 million miles of zeros. Enough zeros to stretch from here to the moon and back over 12 times.

Every thought you think and action you perform requires a complex system of brain cells to fire together. Repeatedly thinking the same thought, saying the same words, visualizing the same image or performing the same action builds a strong inter-connected neural pattern. If you repeatedly dial a friend's phone number, the action will soon be automatic. In your brain, the cells that hold the number are connected to cells associated with your friend. Think of calling that person, and the number pops up immediately. That's because "Neurons that fire together wire together," as neuroscientist Carla Shatz described it.

If you haven't dialed a phone number in a while, the pattern is slow to fire. It's in a dormant file of your brain. You will likely need to stop, concentrate and hope the latent pattern will wake up. If not, you'll need to look up the number. Should you start dialing that number frequently, the pattern will grow stronger and soon you won't have to think about it twice.

Depending upon how often we perform a task or undertake a new one, we are either strengthening dendrites, building new ones or letting them atrophy.

CHANGING THE BRAIN

The fact that dendrites can be grown at any age and that the brain is constantly being reshaped has given rise to the term 'brain plasticity.' Experience, emotion, action, thought change the brain. We discussed that earlier; negative mental patterns can be undone and positive ones established by words, images, shifting our focus, changing our emotional vibration.

The brain demonstrates plasticity in many ways. They rewire to bypass damaged circuits. *In Train Your Mind Change Your Brain*, Sharon Begley writes, "The adult brain, in short, retains much of the plasticity of the developing brain, including the power to repair damaged regions, to grow new neurons, to rezone regions that performed one task and have them assume a new task, to change the circuitry that weaves neurons into the networks that allow us to remember, feel suffer, think, imagine and dream."

We can change the brain and we can grow the brain. Tests were done on taxi drivers in London before and after they studied and learned all the streets in the city. Their brains got bigger! It is a myth that there is a massive loss of brain cells every day after age 30, and mental abilities must decline thereafter. With stimulation, we can even build new brain tissue.

As we age, there are changes in the brain, but overall there is lots of...

GOOD NEWS FOR SENIORS

Even though thinking and reaction time slow down as we age, mental ability remains strong in healthy people. The decline is slight and slow. It affects speed and reaction time, not comprehension. We remain capable of complex thinking, learning and retaining new facts and skills at any age. In one study, 33% of octogenarians scored as well as younger adults on 11 different tests of mental ability.

It may take seniors longer to make decisions, but there is a broader range of knowledge to consider. Consequently, they make better judgments, especially about complex chains of events and human behavior. Older does mean wiser. And usually less selfish, more understanding and tolerant. With age comes a more balanced outlook on life and greater ability to see the humor in it.

The older we are, the more the ability to do several things at once declines. But, as previously mentioned, multi-tasking is really an illusion. It just means attention is jumping around very rapidly. At any age, the brain functions best when focused on one thing at a time. Slow down and focus to improve efficiency and accuracy.

Another positive aspect of aging is what's been called emotional intelligence. With their life experience, seniors are more understanding, better able to judge people and situations, have better control over their emotions and reactions to other people's emotions. In fact, people from 50 – 79 are the least neurotic. Teenagers are the most neurotic. Older people process bad news differently than younger people, and are less responsive to negative information. They are less likely to become depressed by unpleasant happenings.

SUGGESTED READING:
The Brain That Changes Itself by Norman Doidge, M.D.
Mind Power: Rejuvenate Your Brain and Memory Naturally
by Gary Null
The Better Brain Book
by David Perlmutter, M.D. and Carol Colman

MORE INFORMATION: www.dana.org;
www.brainconnection.com;
www.merzenich.positscience.com,
www.bfc.positscience.com, www.cognitivelabs.com

QUOTES TO LIVE BY:

> *The mind, once expanded to the dimensions of larger ideas,*
> *never returns to its original size.*
> — *Oliver Wendell Holmes*

Chapter 20

BRAIN BUILDERS

Think left and think right and think low and think high. Oh, the thinks you can think up if only you try!

Ted Geisel,
a.k.a. Dr. Seuss

The declines in mental performance exhibited by older people are usually the result of negative beliefs about aging and an unhealthy lifestyle. By now, I'm sure, you're exercising, eating lots of fruits and vegetables, drinking water, getting some sun and enough sleep. Add to that mental stimulation, learning, pursuing challenges and new experiences, and you will continue to grow dendrites and maintain brain health. At any age!

Seniors are rapidly disproving the myth that you can't teach an old dog new tricks. They are returning to college in droves, mastering new technologies like computers, cell phones and digital cameras. In fact, more people over 50 are buying computers than any other age group, and 50% of internet users are over 50. People who stay mentally as well as physically active need less medical attention and medication, exhibit better mood and less depression.

Stimulation is health food for the brain. An enriched environment and ongoing learning reduces the risk of brain deterioration, and can keep mind and memory sharp indefinitely. Brains are thrill seekers. They love new, novel, exciting experiences. Try something different, unusual to increase brain activity. Follow the same routine day after day and the brain goes on automatic pilot. Mentally snooze too long and dendrites begin to atrophy.

For an experience to create new neural connections, it must engage your attention, senses, contemplation and action. Simply observing without interacting is not enough. Traveling and exploring, playing games, interacting with people, creating, studying, learning a new skill stimulate the brain. Aging becomes a great adventure, a journey of self-discovery and expansion when you break out of routine, venture into the unknown and tackle challenges.

ASK YOURSELF: What would make me want to jump out of bed in the morning and greet the day with enthusiasm? Be more creative? What would I like to study, learn? Where would I like to go?

Earl Nightingale claimed that 1 hour a day of study in your chosen field of interest makes you a specialist in 3 years, a national authority in 5, and an internationally renowned expert in 7 years.

Four year olds ask an average of 400 questions a day. In meditation, it's called a Beginner's Mind — open and eager. Don't be afraid to be a beginner. Instead of acting like you know it all, try acting like you know nothing. Listen. You'll find life much more interesting.

Today more than ever before, there are extensive opportunities for seniors in travel, education, volunteer work and countless other areas. Libraries and the internet are rich sources of information on every topic imaginable. Not only is losing your mental capacity with age not inevitable, you can improve it. Learn something new every day!

THE LEARNING PROCESS

The average adult retains...

10% of what he READS
20% of what he HEARS
30% of what he SEES
50% of what he HEARS & SEES
70% of what he SAYS
90% of what he SAYS & DOES.

As you can see, retention doesn't come from just reading. To incorporate what we learn, we must use it. Learning is an active 3 step process.

1. EXPERIENCE. First, we have an external experience that is relayed to the brain through the senses. Of all the stimuli in the environment, we only register what we focus on. And that experience is fleeting unless reflected upon.

2. REFLECTION. To imprint and retain something, we must reflect on it — think about what we've experienced, seen, heard, learned. Does it make sense? How does it fit with what I already know? How can I use it?

3. ACTION: Act upon what was learned: put it into practice, solve a problem, use a skill, try something different. Sometimes action is as simple as talking about what was studied or learned.

Knowledge is integrated
— becomes yours — when you act on it.

Unfortunately, we don't always get to Step 2 because we don't have a clear experience to start with. Why? We don't pay attention.

When we see the same things repeatedly, we tend to become mentally lazy. We glance at objects without really seeing them.

A little boy was taken to the seashore for the first time. He was mesmerized. When it came time to leave, his parents kept calling him but he stood at the shore's edge looking out to sea. He heard his parents say, "What is he looking at?" and said to himself, "They look where I look, but they do not see what I see."

We tend to ignore what we've seen many times or what appears dull. I remember one ship we were cruising on as passengers. There was a lady traveling by herself. She was fairly old, didn't wear makeup and wore dark dresses without any style. If it weren't for the fact that it was a rather small ship, I would not have noticed her. At some point someone mentioned that this woman's family had started that cruise line. My interest was immediately aroused. What a fascinating story she must have to tell! Unfortunately, I did not get the opportunity to meet her, but I remember the incident because it demonstrated how quickly perception can shift from bored to interested.

Interest wakes up the brain. It's a brain stimulant. But when we dismiss something or someone as dull, we miss the potential treasure behind the façade. People or things that are unique, different, have distinguishing characteristics, are attention grabbers. But we can stimulate interest with concentration. Interest naturally produces concentration but concentration produces interest. Take the time to observe, probe, explore, question, and you will be richly rewarded.

To train yourself to concentrate and be more observant…

Pick up a magazine and find a full page picture. Don't choose one that is exciting and interesting. Look for the opposite, something uninteresting. Concentrate on the picture for about 20 seconds. Observe as much as you can. Since the picture is dull, be aware of the mind's desire to wander, but stay focused and absorb as much as possible.

Turn the picture face down, pick up a pen and write down everything you remember about the picture. What did you notice — items, people, colors, design? What do you think of the picture? What was its purpose? How would you describe it to someone else? Then go back and see what you missed.

If I hadn't asked you to concentrate on such a picture, you probably would have flipped right past it in the magazine. And you wouldn't have recalled anything about it. **No attention = no retention.** But because you paid attention, you discovered some interesting things, didn't you? Concentration reveals information we would normally miss.

Interest produces concentration
BUT concentration produces interest.

Concentration and observation are essential to learning. They automatically put the mind in a learning and remembering mode. The more we concentrate, the more the brain tunes into what we're doing and imprints it. We also learn faster and remember more when we can associate new knowledge with what we already know. The new information hooks into an established neural pattern. If it has to form a whole new network, the information will need to be repeated and used frequently until the synaptic connections are established.

Our minds are very busy. Paying attention, concentrating for any length of time isn't the easiest thing in the world. But they are skills that can be developed and strengthened. There are things you can do to…

ENHANCE LEARNING

Deep breathing and exercise fuel the brain with oxygen.

Meditation releases stress, clears the mind and inspires creative thinking.

Retention is better if we read/study for two $^1/_2$ hour sessions rather than one hour straight.

Focus on material for a short period (**EXPERIENCE**), think about it (**REFLECT**), and use it (**ACT**) before going on.

Focus 100%. Avoid interruptions and distractions. It can take up to 15 minutes to regain full concentration after losing it.

Determine what is worth learning and remembering and what isn't.

Focus on key ideas and things you don't already know. Use highlighter. Take notes.

Review immediately after reading. Restate the message in your own words. Write about what you've learned.

Get a good sleep. The brain integrates newly learned information during sleep. What you want to retain is best reviewed just before sleep.

Experience — the first step in learning — is acquired through the senses. Develop your five senses (see next chapter).

Associate what you learn with what you already know.

Ask yourself questions while reading. What is this about? How does it apply to me? What can I do with this information?

Place yourself in a scene. Vividly imagine what you're reading.

Train yourself to notice details.

Refresh your memories. Mentally review what you learned over the coming days.

Learning builds dendrites and protects against Alzheimer's. Learning a musical instrument or a new language are particularly good dendrite builders. Travel is mentally and socially stimulating. It provides novelty and breaks us out of routine. We build dendrites when we explore new places, study cultures and customs, endeavor to communicate in another language.

The world is a book and those who do not travel read only one page.
— St. Augustine

There are many other...

DENDRITE BUILDERS

1. Activities like juggling and dancing that require combining concentration, rhythm and movement. Juggling activates both hemispheres of the brain. Just throwing and catching a single ball improves hand-eye coordination and has a positive affect on the brain.

2. Keep challenging yourself. Once you've mastered something, take it to the next level. It's the challenge that benefits most.

3. Use all your skills and senses.

4. Solve problems. Complexity places demands on various abilities and parts of the brain.

5. Make your life fun and interesting. Change your routine. Break set patterns and create new ones. Alter the order in which you do things. Explore. Walk or drive different routes.

6. Reward yourself. Rewards release chemicals in the brain that make us feel good, and increase the desire to learn and the ability to remember.

7. Socialize. Put yourself in social settings where you will meet new people, learn new information and be stimulated by conversation.

8. Play word games, crossword puzzles, anagrams. Make words from words. Try to think of different colors, flowers, countries, cars etc. that start with each letter of the alphabet. Rewrite common cliches. What else could you describe as cool besides a cucumber?

Sweet as	Slow as
Cool as	Sour as
Slippery as	Red as

9. Play challenging games, ones that force you to think ahead and strategize. Chess, checkers, backgammon, card games.

10. Solve puzzles like brain twisters and sudoku.

11. Solve riddles. They stir the imagination and make us look at things from different angles, think outside the box.

I like nonsense; it wakes up the brain cells.

– Dr. Seuss

Try these…

A. You are in a foot race and overtake the person in second place. What position are you in?

B. There is one word in the English language that is always pronounced incorrectly. What is it?

C. How many animals of each sex did Moses take on the ark?

D. Is a man allowed to marry his widow's sister?

E. Mary's father has five daughters: Nana, Nene, Nini, Nono. What is the name of the fifth daughter?

See answers at the end of this chapter.

12. Daydream. Imagination stimulates the brain and nervous system.

13. Strengthen the non-dominant part of your brain and rarely used neural pathways by using your non-dominant hand to do common tasks like brushing your teeth, eating, combing your hair.

    EXERCISE: Raise your dominant hand. In the air, write the word ghost. Easy, right? Now raise your non-dominant hand and write the same word.

What was the difference? You had to think, didn't you? You woke up the dormant hemisphere of your brain and activated a whole different set of neural circuits.

Certain activities like these are proven dendrite builders. Boredom causes a decline in mental acuity. Be on guard against your brain running on automatic pilot. It loves to make assumptions, jump to conclusions and react without thinking because then it gets to snooze. And you know the saying: You snooze, you lose! Dendrites that is.

ANSWERS TO RIDDLES:

A. If you overtake the second person and take his place, you are in second place.

B. Incorrectly.

C. None. Noah took animals on the ark.

D. Only if there's marriage in heaven. If the man's wife is a widow, the man is dead.

E. Nunu? No, no! The fifth daughter's name is Mary.

SUGGESTED READING: *The Art Of Changing The Brain* by James E. Zull

MORE INFORMATION: www.elderhostel.org; www.seniornet.org; www.ezinearticles.com; www.puzzles.com; www.thinks.com; www.increasebrainpower.com

For a small onetime fee, www.knowledgenews.net will send you daily information on an array of topics — history, geology, politics, culture to name a few.

QUOTES TO LIVE BY:

> *Unless you try to do something beyond*
> *what you have already mastered, you will never grow.*
> — *Ralph Waldo Emerson*

Chapter 21

BE SENSE-ABLE

I go to nature to be soothed and healed, and to have my senses put in order.

John Burroughs

Our entire experience of the external world is transferred to our brains via the five senses. 80-90% of that incoming information is visual. Such strong reliance on sight has resulted in the suppression of the other senses.

That's unfortunate because the more senses associated with an experience...

> The more knowledge acquired
> The greater the brain stimulus
> The more neural pathways created
> The stronger the network formed
> The greater the imprint
> The easier to retrieve the memory.

Using all the senses builds greater dendritic patterns, activates multiple areas of the brain and expands memory. If one neural network should be blocked due to stroke or brain injury, information could still be retrieved from other brain regions. If sight were lost, for instance, we would still recognize a rose by touch and smell.

When a person loses one sense faculty, and that area of the brain is no longer in use, other faculties move in and take over that space. This is one of the most interesting discoveries about the brain in recent years. We are not hardwired from birth. The brain is plastic throughout life, but especially in childhood.

Each sense stimulates a different region of the brain. Silently reading uses one part of the brain. Read aloud and other areas are activated. Write words and still other parts of the brain come into play. One reason children learn so much, so fast is that they explore the world with all their senses. They look at an object, feel it, smell it, try to taste it, shake it for sound. An infant has twice as many dendrites as an adult. That number gradually diminishes until adolescence. At the same time, we start relying more on sight and less on the other senses.

Closing off one sense automatically increases the attention and awareness of the others. Not only will waking up all our senses be good for the brain, it will enhance our experience of life. Taking a walk outdoors is a whole different and wonderful adventure when you hold someone's hand and walk with eyes closed. For one thing, you will be much more aware of the smells in the air.

SMELL

The sense of smell can be extraordinarily evocative,
bringing back pictures as sharp as photographs of scenes
that had left the conscious mind.
— *Thalassa Cruso*

Our least used sense is that of smell, but it is the most acute. Humans can discern the difference between 4,000 to 10,000 different scents. A dog's sense of smell is 100 times greater than that. Potent smells form fast and firm imprints on the brain. Infants bond with their mothers primarily through smell. Scents connect to long term memory and resonate forgotten memories.

When I smell fresh mown hay, I am instantly transported back to childhood summers in Vermont.

The primary odors are camphoric (mothballs), musky (perfume), roses, peppermint, etheral (dry cleaning fluid), pungent (vinegar), putrid (rotten eggs). Practice identifying different scents. What sensations do they arouse? Close your eyes throughout the day and try to detect the different odors in the atmosphere. Smell your food before eating it. Notice how different smells affect you. Aroma therapy is based on the healing power of different scents.

Various research projects have studied the effects of specific scents. The smell of cinnamon had positive affects on brainpower.

Peppermint has been linked to higher energy levels and better brain performance. One research project found that the smell of peppermint improved mood and motivation, and had a positive affect on athletic performance.

The strength of the sense of smell declines with age but complete loss of smell may be a sign of the onset of dementia. Smelling and tasting are closely connected.

TASTE

Sour, sweet, bitter, pungent, all must be tasted.
— Chinese proverb

About 80-90% of what we think is taste is actually due to smell. There are almost 10,000 buds in the mouth and a single taste bud has 50 – 100 taste cells. Nevertheless, taste is the weakest of the human senses and as we age, our taste buds become less sensitive.

Tastes fall into four categories: salty, sour, sweet and bitter. Close your eyes when you eat and savor the taste of the food. If we would stop to really taste food, we would enjoy eating more and probably consume less. To develop your sense of taste, have someone present you with small bites of different foods and see if you can identify them. When you eat or drink something, try to distinguish between the flavors in it. What feelings do different tastes arouse?

TOUCH

Kindness is more than deeds. It is an attitude,
an expression, a look, a touch.
— *Anonymous*

Skin is the body's largest organ accounting for 12 - 15% of total body weight. It can weigh over twelve pounds. The thousands of nerve endings inside every square inch of skin send messages to the brain related to everything we touch. Hands, lips, face, neck, tongue, fingertips and feet are the most sensitive to touch. How do you feel? Literally. What is the texture, color, smoothness of your skin?

We learn by touching, taking apart, getting the feel for something. Physical touch is crucial to well-being. Experiments on animals proved that those who received affection and physical contact had healthier, longer lives. A touch, a hug, a warm handshake or pat on the back can convey more than words.

Touch those close to you. Hug, hold hands, kiss. How do people feel? How do you feel when someone touches you? Close your eyes and have a person put different objects in your hands. Describe the sensations, the texture and shape of each. Try to identify it. Close your eyes while taking a bath or a shower. Experience the feel of the water on your body. Locate soap and shampoo with your eyes closed. Have a massage and focus on the different tactile sensations. A woman's skin is much thinner and more sensitive to touch than men. A woman can find a certain degree of pressure uncomfortable that a man hardly feels at all.

Skin reveals a lot about a person's health and emotions. Fever or embarrassment make the skin sweat or flush. Toxins pass through the skin going in and coming out. Even though our outer layer of skin — the epidermis — is totally replaced about every 28 - 30 days, it loses tone, elasticity and firmness due to constant exposure to pollutants and the elements. Internal problems also affect the skin. Inflammation, stress, poor nutrition, toxins, allergies are likely to reveal themselves on the skin. Complexions can glow with health or reflect internal disorders. If you don't drink enough water or get enough sleep, it will soon be evident on your face. The skin sags and loses color.

HEARING

The quieter you become, the more you can hear.
— *Baba Ramdas*

What we call sound is a vibration in the ear. It turns into electrical impulses that travel to the brain. Sounds vary according to pitch, rhythm and tone. Women have better hearing than men. Children have more sensitive ears than adults. They can recognize a wider variety of noises. Most animals have a good sense of hearing, better than humans.

Hearing becomes sharper in people who lose their sight. By closing your eyes throughout the day and listening, you can sharpen your auditory sense. Sit down in a mall or on park bench, close your eyes and try to distinguish between the various sounds. Listen to the television with your eyes closed and try to discern the emotions being expressed by the speaker's tone of voice. Close your eyes while talking on the telephone.

Notice the feelings and fluctuations in people's voices. What voices sound the most pleasing to you. Male/female? High/low? Intense/soft?

Play different types of music. Note the physiological response in your body. How does it affect your thinking, your emotions? Attentive listening increases understanding and thinking as well as memory.

SIGHT

The eyes are the most refined of our senses, the one which communicates most directly with our mind, our consciousness.
— Robert Delaunay

35% of brain volume is devoted to eyesight. We learn best by seeing, but unfortunately we aren't using our eyesight to its fullest capacity. Like the little boy at the shore, we look without seeing. The brain receives an image of the things we look at it but it doesn't retain or learn from them unless we concentrate.

We can increase observational skills by studying a scene inside or outside the house, closing our eyes and recreating it in our minds. Incorporate size, shape and colors into your mental image. Then open your eyes and note how accurate you were.

We can improve our ability to read body language by blocking out sound. My husband and I traveled around the U.S. and Canada for 6 years in a large motor home. In the days before satellite television, there were areas in Canada where we only picked up French programs. He was able to enjoy watching an entire movie without sound, just imagining from the scenes and body language what was going on.

NOTE: Loss of eyesight is one of the greatest fears of people as they age. In the United States, macular degeneration is the leading cause of blindness. Once again, we must turn to good nutrition, supplements and exercise to prevent degeneration. Lutein, Vitamin A and fish oil are highly recommended for the eyes. Some books you might wish to refer to: *The Eye Care Revolution:*

Prevent and Reverse Common Vision Problems by Robert Abel, Jr., MD. Natural Eye Care: An Encyclopedia by Marc Grossman, OD, LAc, and Glen Swartwoud, OD.

* * * * * *

The more senses involved in learning or experiencing something, the more active the brain, the greater the memory imprint. If you want to increase the likelihood of remembering what you are reading, invoke your auditory sense by reading it aloud or your sense of touch by writing it down. Images are easier to recall than words. Even boring facts can be retained if put into a symbolic image.

Become aware of your learning preference. Visual learners think in images and learn best with visual aids: pictures, diagrams, charts, slides, movies, color. Auditory people like to hear information via lectures, tapes, discussions. They learn best by listening or speaking. Things that sound pleasant, have rhythm or rhyme or alliteration are easier to remember. Kinesthetics learn best by doing. The like to be physically involved, touch things, take them apart and put them back together.

WAKE UP YOUR SENSES. What senses are activated when you think of: a carnation, pastrami, soap, beer, paper, sand, fire, ice, the zoo, a river, a lemon, silk, vanilla, cinnamon, mud, trash, snow, a puppy, cotton candy, a train, a kaleidoscope, sour milk, hair.

SUGGESTED READING:
Easy Genius: Awakening Your Whole Brain to Build a More Powerful Memory by Chance Massaro and Steve Wallis

MORE INFORMATION: discovermagazine.com
(Under search, type senses.)

QUOTES TO LIVE BY:

Our senses are indeed our doors and windows on this world,
In a very real sense the key to the unlocking of meaning
and the wellspring of creativity.

— *Jean Houston*

Chapter 22

MEMORIES ARE MADE OF THIS

Memory... is the diary that we all carry about with us.

Oscar Wilde

After age 70, your memory retrieval rate may diminish by about 10%. That doesn't mean you're losing your memory! It just takes longer to pull information from the files. That happened to me recently when I ran into an old friend. Try as I did, I couldn't recall his name. Believing honesty to be the best policy in such situations, I confessed…

"Don't worry about it," he told me. "Happens to me all the time. I finally took a memory course."

"Did it help?" I asked.

"Oh, yes. It taught me to associate things. That helps you remember. You might want to try it."

"What was the name of the course?" I asked.

"You know the flower with the long stem and the thorns?"

"Rose," I said.

"That's right," he nodded. He then turned toward his wife and called out, "Hey, Rose. What was the name of that memory course I took?"

There are a lot of variations on that joke, and while we may laugh at them, there is always a little anxiety behind the laughter. Am I losing it? Is this the beginning of the dreaded 'A' word?

Losing things happens to everyone at every stage of life, but after a certain age misplacing keys can cause an anxiety attack. Fear of Alzheimer's Disease can make us over-react to normal memory lapses.

If your memory really is slipping, it is not necessarily due to dementia. Memory and cognitive function in older people are affected by...

Poor nutrition due to smaller appetite
Isolation due to shrinking social circles
Less mental stimulation due to poor eyesight/hearing
Less exercise due to disease, physical impairment.

For the most part, these problems are correctable. As you know by now, we can protect and even improve brain and memory with physical and mental exercise. In addition, understanding the mechanics of memory, what influences it, how we remember and why we forget will help us make better use of this amazing faculty.

Memory and remembering are not the same. Remembering is a process that imprints information on the brain, stores and retrieves it. It is an action, therefore a verb. Memory is a noun because it is a thing — a picture, feeling, capsule of information. Remembering is similar to entering information into a computer, saving it and then hitting a few keys when you want to retrieve it. What's saved is called a memory.

Unlike a computer's memory, ours is not located in one place. It permeates the body, the central nervous system, the immune system and the cells. While the brain is responsible for the mechanics of remembering, memory itself cannot be isolated.

Biochemist Candace Pert proved that intelligence and memories are not confined to the brain but run through the entire body-mind network of cells and molecules. In her book, Molecules of Emotion, she writes, "Every second, a massive information exchange is occurring in your body."

Everything we experience, think, sense and feel affects the whole body-mind. But not everything has enough impact to form a memory. We are constantly exposed to thousands of sensory stimuli but ignore most of it. Some things receive fleeting attention, others we focus on a little while, then forget, and some we hold onto.

To better understand how memory functions, picture it as three different file cabinets: *The Sensory File, Working File* and *Long-term File*.

THE SENSORY FILE

The Sensory File registers immediate sensory data: the sights, experiences, sounds, smells etc. we're constantly bombarded with. We filter that massive amount of sensory stimuli and allow only a few things into awareness, probably less than 1%. And that's quickly pushed aside if something else makes a stronger impression. The Sensory File is like a blackboard we constantly erase and write over.

You may be taking a walk enjoying the sound of birds chirping when suddenly a car screeches to a halt. Your ears immediately block out the birds and focus on the screeching brakes. You clearly hear the angry voices of the drivers until your cell phone rings. Then you block them out. Your spouse is on the phone asking you to stop at the store and pick up some milk. Now there's something you must remember to do. The Sensory File is no longer sufficient. When further thought or action is required, we use the Short-term or Working File.

THE SHORT TERM/WORKING FILE

This is where we do thinking in the moment like figuring out a math problem or hold tasks we must remember to do in the immediate future. The Working File holds information for the amount of time it is needed in the present. It's analogous to a temporary holding area. We use it to block out interference so we can focus, think, analyze, act. Anything given less than one minute of attention will fade from memory. I'm sure you've experienced that by repeating a phone number until you dialed it and then promptly forgetting it.

Following is a process that requires using short-term memory. Notice how you must block everything else from your mind to be able to focus and follow the steps. Also, notice how quickly you forget one step as your mind moves on to the next. Do this in your head, no paper and pencil, and choose the first answer that comes to mind.

1. Pick a number from 2 to 9. It can be 2 or 9 or any number in between.

2. Take the number you've chosen, and multiply it by 9.

3. That should give you a two digit number. Take those two digits and add them together.

4. Take the resulting number and subtract 5 from it.

5. Take that number and correspond it to letters in the alphabet by numbering the letters…
   A = 1, B = 2, C = 3, D = 4 etc.

6. Think of a country that begins with that letter, the first that comes to mind.

7. Take the last letter in the name of that country, and think of an animal. Again, the first that comes to mind.

8. Now take the last letter in the name of that animal, and think of a color.

9. What color, animal and country are you thinking of?

Notice that short-term memory is limited in what it can concentrate on. At best, most people can only hold seven things in conscious awareness at any moment. As you changed focus from one step to the next, you quickly forgot the preceding step. Oh, by the way, there are no orange kangaroos in Denmark.

If we're not careful, what's in our working file can easily be bumped off center stage by something else. How many times have you answered the phone, talked a couple of minutes, hung up and said to yourself, "Now what was I just doing?" This is where most people have problems as they age — with short-term memory.

Three sisters in their 90s lived together. They were in pretty good health but losing their memories. One was 90, one 93 and the oldest 95.

The oldest went upstairs one evening to take a bath. As she was getting in the tub with one foot in and one foot out, she called down to her sisters, "Am I getting in the tub or am I getting out of the tub?"

The 93 year old decided to go upstairs and see if she could help figure out the situation. She got half way up, stopped to catch her breath, looked around and called out, "Am I going up the stairs or am I coming down the stairs?"

The 90 year old rapped her knuckles on the kitchen table and said, "Knock wood. I hope my memory never gets as bad as my sisters'." Then she stood up and said, "Now was that a knock at the front door or the back?"

Nothing stays in the Working File unless it's working. We need to keep paying attention or it slips away to be replaced by something else. Barring health problems, the reason most people have difficulty with short-term memory is not that their memory is failing but because they are not paying attention. Most of us don't fully focus on what's happening in the present moment. We're easily distracted or we think we already know something so we don't pay attention. In addition, we overload the Working File by trying to think about and do too many things at once.

LONG TERM FILE

If we give something enough attention, meaning or emotion, it will automatically go from the Working File to the Long-term File. This is where we hold the vast amount of skill and information we have acquired over a lifetime: general knowledge and facts, skills we possess like tying shoes, riding a bike, swimming, and the personal story of our lives.

The mind can hold an infinite amount of long-term memory under normal conditions. Whether we can retrieve it or not depends on how great an impact it made and how often we use that information. For something to register in long-term memory, it must have impact. That means…

EMOTIONAL EFFECT

The more emotional an experience, the greater its impact on the brain and the stronger the memory. To demonstrate the difference between an experience that arouses emotions and one that doesn't…

Imagine you are driving home from the store and an ambulance passes you, lights flashing, siren wailing. That's happened to all of us. No big deal. But then you notice that the ambulance has turned down your street. You are instantly more alert, interested. You hasten to drive the next two blocks and turn down your street.

The ambulance has stopped in front of your apartment building. How do you feel?

When you see the ambulance in front of your building, emotions are aroused. Even if your family and neighbors are okay, you will remember the incident for some time because it had an emotional impact.

Go back in your memory bank and pull up something that had a strong, positive emotional effect on you. Perhaps your wedding day, the birth of a child, seeing a loved one after a long absence. Notice how quickly the memory rushes forward and the intricacy of it. Lots of brain cells are firing together to produce multiple images connected to that emotional experience. Neural patterns formed by emotion remain long after the event that created them. Those formed by deep emotion are the strongest and hardest to dissolve.

PSYCHOLOGICAL EFFECT

Who was the teacher who had the most influence on you in school? Have you ever had an experience that changed your thinking about yourself, other people, the world? What were the defining moments of your life? Anything that has a powerful psychological impact on us creates a strong memory.

In 2002, my husband and I took a world cruise. It was one of the highlights of my life. I remember many of the ports vividly because seeing how the rest of the world lives greatly affected my thinking and world view.

PHYSICAL EFFECT

Physical pain also has a strong impact on the brain. If you were hit in the face by a wayward Frisbee on the beach, the memory would be triggered whenever you saw one, and your body would respond with tension and alertness.

Survival depends on remembering what can hurt us. We only need to be burned once to remember that fire burns. People can recount every detail of a serious illness or accident they had.

Advertisers try to arouse pleasant emotional and physical sensations so we'll be more likely to remember and buy their product. Politicians hope to have a psychological impact on us

INTEREST

Each day is filled with interesting events and experiences, but we don't pay attention unless they are of interest to us personally. Consequently, they don't register. Your mind doesn't take seriously what you don't pay attention to and doesn't bother to create a memory. NO ATTENTION = NO RETENTION. As previously mentioned, however, we can arouse interest and thus register and retain much more of what we are exposed to.

* * * * * *

We naturally remember people, events and experiences that impact us in some way, but what we remember and what actually happened are often two different things.

> *The past is malleable and flexible, changing as our recollection interprets and re-explains what has happened.*
> *– Peter Berger*

Our memories are colored by our individuality. Our unique background, conditioning and beliefs create a filter through which we see and interpret life. That's why people witnessing the same incident often give conflicting accounts. They have different perceptual filters. What you pick up from the surrounding environment may be entirely different from what I pick up. Past experience and conditioning affect what we perceive and record. People who grow up in a hostile environment are hyper-alert to signs of threat and may sense aggression where the next person does not.

Your personal experience and therefore your memory of an event is determined by your background, conditioning, senses, judgments and values. What you are thinking and feeling right now affect how the nature of your memories. Since our thoughts and feelings change, memories change.

Some of the factors that influence and change memories...

SUGGESTION

Did you ever have someone mention an incident and say, "You remember that, don't you?" You don't, but as they continue to describe it, you start to think maybe you do. The power of suggestion can lead us to make up a memory. Children may hear a family story so many times they think they were there even if it actually occurred before they were born. The power of suggestion affects memories as well as thinking.

The way a question is posed can affect the way we remember something. The words used, the attitude of the questioner, the reason for the question can affect our thinking and plant a suggestion as to how we answer.

> *The fault with old men's memories is that they remember*
> *so many things that ain't so.*
> *– Mark Twain*

EXPECTATION

Information received before or after an event can enter into one's perception and interpretation. Perhaps you spoke to someone in the hallway before a conference and later mistakenly believed that person was at the conference because you expected her to be.

PREFERENCE

Memories are stories and as such they often fall into the category of fiction. In weaving a memory-story, people edit what happened to correspond with their self-image and perception. Their present emotional and psychological state have an affect. We even add details that weren't part of the actual event. This is unconscious and happens for two reasons. One is that we only remember the highlights of an event, not the details. The brain weaves the highlights together into a reasonable story by filling in the blanks. We also edit memories to adjust to our personal version of reality. The way we want to remember something can be very different from what actually happened. That's why there is the actual event and the remembered event, and sometimes the two don't have much in common.

Let us admit that there are two histories, the actual series of events that once occurred; and the ideal series that we affirm and hold in memory.
– Carl Becker

The fact is... MEMORIES ARE MADE OF YOU!

Memory is subjective. Your memories are a reflection of you and you are a reflection of your memories. Your disposition, personal experience, conditioning, thoughts, emotions and attitude all color your memories. Memories are malleable. Perspective changes with every experience and thus memories change. In creating our personal memories, it is easy to confuse or merge different situations or past and present into one story.

Memories even change based on the mood we're in. Your emotional, physical and psychological condition at any given time dictate what you remember and how you remember it. This is called…

STATE DEPENDENT MEMORY

MEMORY REACTS TO:

Environment
Thoughts and Attitude
Physical state
Emotions.

Return to a place you've been before and the environment stimulates memories of previous experiences there. When we took my mother out to eat, she enjoyed it, but by the time we took her back to the nursing home, she had forgotten where we were, couldn't describe anything about the place or what she ate. But when we returned to that restaurant, even if it was months later, she'd say, "Oh, we've been here before." The environment stimulated the memory.

Physical conditions also trigger state dependent memory. When you have a particular physical experience, memories of corresponding experiences will be triggered. In 2002, during a bicycle tour in France, I fell and broke my pelvis. Fortunately, I healed well and a few months later, I was rollerblading. My skate hit something and I fell again. My body followed the same trajectory it had when I fell off the bike. This fall wasn't serious, I wasn't hurt, but as I was going down, my mind vividly replayed the bicycle fall. This was due to state dependent memory — being in the same or a similar physical state.

State dependent memory also applies to emotional and psychological states. This was proved by an interesting test performed on college students. Results showed that material studied when drunk was best recalled when drunk. Those who studied drunk but tested sober didn't do nearly as well as those who studied and were tested in the same condition. Not that it's good to study and take tests in a drunken state! Students who were sober during learning and testing did better than their tipsy counterparts.

The way you feel right now, the mood you're in, affects what you remember and how you remember it. Your mood also influences how you perceive the future. Being in a particular mood tunes you into a corresponding wavelength in your mind. All the memories and images of other times you were in the same state are running on that channel. The neurons holding similar, associated memories are triggered. Biochemist Candace Pert writes, "Positive emotional experiences are much more likely to be recalled when we're in an upbeat mood, while negative emotional experiences are recalled more easily when we're already in a bad mood."

That's why slight irritation can quickly escalate into rage. We tune into the angry channel, and past memories and angry feelings bubble to the surface and burst. Similarly, we can start out feeling a little sad or guilty and soon be overwhelmed by those feelings. It's as if we opened Pandora's Box.

What to do in such situations? By the power of choice, you can turn your attention to a positive emotion, a pleasant scene, a good memory and focus on it until you literally change channels, tune into an entirely different vibration of energy and wake up different neural patterns.

As moods affect memory, so do thoughts and attitude…

There is more memory loss among people who live in countries with a negative cultural attitude toward aging and the elderly.

Believing memory fails with age is a self-fulfilling prophesy.

Thinking and memory improve when you're happy.

A positive attitude is not only good for your health, it's good for your memory. Confidence in your mind and memory helps them function at their best. Expecting to be forgetful is almost a guarantee that you will be. But there are other reasons for forgetting as well.

WHY WE FORGET

Forgetting is defined as the loss of information over time. Unused knowledge and information tends to be discarded. In some cases, this is beneficial. We need to clear our memory banks of useless information to make room for new memories. When a friend moves and gets a new telephone number, we need to update our memory bank, erase the old number so we can learn and remember the new one. We automatically prioritize information, quickly forgetting things we regard as irrelevant and unimportant so we can focus on more important matters. But even when we are interested and paying attention, we can lose our train of thought and forget if we're distracted.

Some forgetfulness is due to repression. Repression hides from conscious awareness things we find too painful to face. We are inclined to purposely forget unresolved problems, unhealed emotions and experiences that threaten our self-image because we don't want to recall them. They are too painful and we don't know how to deal with them. Unfortunately, repression doesn't make problems disappear. Add memory impairment to the emotional and physical problems repression can cause. I am convinced that my mother developed dementia because she willed herself to forget a particularly painful experience. I can't count the number of times I heard her say, "If I could just erase that from my memory." Eventually, she did. But her desire to forget affected more than that one experience.

Nothing has a worse affect on memory than stress. We take in less oxygen when we're stressed and that impairs brain function. Chronic stress inhibits learning and is deadly to memory centers of the brain. Information overload stresses and shrinks the brain.

Learning and remembering improve 50% or more in people who are not stressed.

A cluttered mind is forgetful. Are your thoughts wandering? Are you trying to do several things at once? Do you expect to forget? If difficulty in recording, retaining and retrieving memories arises suddenly, the first thing to check is the side effects of your drugs. Memories of frequently repeated activities jumble together. You probably can't remember what you had for dinner last night without really thinking about it unless you had something different from the norm or ate in a different locale. Just because you don't quickly recall what you had for dinner doesn't mean you're losing your memory.

Health, sleep, attitude, mood, social skills, and how often we use information all affect our ability to remember. If you recall something one day and forget it the next, it could be that your blood sugar is low or you're depressed. Depression affects brain chemistry and memory. And don't forget the importance of exercise in keeping the brain supplied with oxygen. A sluggish brain means a poor memory.

All that being said, the main reason we forget is simple. We're not paying attention.

A retired man came home from his morning walk.

"How was your walk?" asked his wife.

"Rather strange," he said. "I ran into Bob Jones along the way and said, 'Hello, Jones. How are you doing?'"

"'Not too bad,' he said. 'And you, Smith? How are you?'" "My name's not Smith,' I told him."

"'I guess we're even then,' he told me, 'because mine's not Jones.'"

"We took a closer look and sure enough, it was neither of us.'"
Don't *forget* what affects aging more than anything else. Attitude.

MEMORY BLOCKERS

Negative attitude, stress, repression and depression
Illness, fatigue
Malnutrition
Distractions, loud environments
All affect the brain, slow absorption of information.

Be careful if you are taking statins to lower cholesterol. They could be significantly affecting your memory and not in a good way. The brain needs good cholesterol.

SUGGESTED READING: *Your Memory: How It Works and How to Improve It* by Kenneth L. Higbee

QUOTES TO LIVE BY:

Memory is history recorded in our brain, memory is a painter, it paints pictures of the past and of the day.
— *Anna Mary Robertson Moses (Grandma Moses)*

Chapter 23

MEMORY METHODS

"The horror of that moment," the king went on, "I shall never, never forget!"
"You will though," the queen said, "if you don't make a memorandum of it."

Lewis Carroll

Now that we know the mechanics of memory, let's look at how we can improve memory skills which, by the way, can raise IQ. Learning and memory are closely related. New, unusual, challenging activities not only build the brain, they strengthen memory.

Within an hour of an occurrence, we either forget or file it in long-term memory. Much of what we call memory loss is simply not paying attention. I can't say this often enough: No attention means no retention. As we've just seen, we easily recall experiences that affect us physically, psychologically or emotionally. With the following techniques, we can increase our ability to retain and retrieve anything.

REPETITION I'm sure you remember your school days and how many things you had to learn through repetition. Constantly repeating something is not the most pleasant way to learn, but it does drill information into our brains. We form memories of what we hear repeatedly. The more a word or thought or experience is repeated, the deeper the neural circuit it carves.

Repetitive action is the best way to learn a skill. Mental or verbal repetition is the best way to hold information in the short-term memory. But if you want to retain information, other strategies work better.

ASSOCIATION

Imagine that you are on a cruise ship and one of your table mates happens to be a physicist. At dinner, he starts talking about quarks and waves and particles. You're totally baffled and bored, and he knows it. The next night he arrives with pictures, puts his message in a context you can relate to and understand. Suddenly you're all eyes and ears! You grasp what he is talking about and are able to recall it later. That's because the physicist associated what he was teaching you with what you already knew.

The brain naturally tries to associate new information and sensory input with previously established neural patterns. When you arrive in a place for the first time, don't you find yourself saying, "This reminds me of..." Or, you associate a new acquaintance with someone who looks or sounds similar. We connect names of people we meet with people we know. On occasion, this can lead to problems...

A new man in town went to the local supermarket to grocery shop. The cashier greeted him, "Hello, Mr. Black." The man smiled and said, "I'm afraid I am not Mr. Black. My name is Rogers." When he returned to the market the following week, the cashier greeted him enthusiastically, "Oh, Mr. Black, you're not going to believe this, but there's a man who comes in here who looks just like you."

When putting information into your memory bank, try to connect it to existing neural networks. Link it or recode it into something familiar. Recoding is a method of association. By creating an acronym, for instance, you translate something you want to remember into something you already know. HOMES is an acronym for recalling the names of the Great Lakes. It contains the first initial of each word — Huron, Ontario, Michigan, Erie and Superior. The letters in Homes act as retrieval clues for the full words.

The best associations are those made with the familiar, meaningful or funny. The more associations, the wider the neural network and the better the memory.

VISUALIZATION

As you know, at least 80% of sensory input is visual. The mind thinks primarily in images. That's why it's easier to remember faces than names. If you can envision what you're reading or learning, it will make a stronger memory impression.

STORIES

Stories are the most powerful memory technique of all because memory is story based. The sillier, the funnier, the livelier the story, the stronger the memory. But stories must have logical continuity, one image triggering the next.

The most memorable stories incorporate…

SENSES. The more sensual affects you add to your story, the more neurons involved and the greater the memory trace.

IMAGINATION. Use your imagination to create vivid stories. We are more likely to review and remember stories that are colorful, active and interesting.

EXAGGERATION. Research has shown that we recall things that are unusual and peculiar. The sillier, funnier or more outlandish a story is, the easier it is to remember.

RATIONAL ORDER. Interacting images provide flow to a story and make it easier to remember than a list of individual items. Use continuous, logical sequence so that one image naturally triggers the next one.

Now let's do a little memory test...

EXERCISE:

1. Below are 7 unrelated words. Study them for 15 seconds using just repetition in an effort to remember them. Then cover the words.

ELEPHANT
VIOLIN
HAIR DRYER
TELEPHONE
ICE CREAM
TUXEDO
BOOK.

2. Relax, take a few deep breaths and write down as many of the words as you can recall. Check your answers.

Unless you have a very good memory, you won't remember these words using just repetition — especially after a little time elapses. Most people can't hold more than 7 things in their short-term memory at any given moment. In an exercise like this, it would not be uncommon to only remember 3 − 5 of the words. As time goes by, the memory would fade.

3. Look at the 7 items again and create a story. Make it visual, silly, funny, active, colorful. Just be sure there is some rhyme and reason to the story, that one picture triggers the next. Review your story and then turn the paper over.

4. Relax, take a few deep breaths. Now try to remember the 7 words. Write them down and check your answers.

Here's a sample story using the 7 words...

An ELEPHANT wearing a TUXEDO was playing the VIOLIN. He had an ICE CREAM stain on his shirt which his wife was trying to remove with a HAIR DRYER. She had to stand on a TELEPHONE BOOK to reach it.

After I do a similar exercise during my lectures on ships, people approach me for days repeating the story and the 7 items. One time a lady blamed me for not being able to fall asleep for hours one night because she couldn't remember the seventh item. "Finally, it came to me," she laughed, "and I fell right to sleep."

Most people don't need to remember a large number of unrelated things. But these techniques strengthen the brain and memory. When you do want to remember something, focus in on what is important, emotional or novel about it. When linking many things, use motion, humor and color to create the most memorable stories.

I have a girlfriend who has a wonderful memory because she is a great storyteller. When Helene recounts an experience, she makes you feel like you're right there. She injects emotion and action into the telling and makes it all come alive with vivid descriptions of color, sights and sounds. Talk about the power of suggestion. If you've heard any of her stories several times, you start to think maybe you were there!

* * * * * *

NAMES

One of the benefits of travel is meeting people and making new friends. One of the greatest challenges is remembering their names.

> I never forget a face or a name;
> The bothersome thing in my case is:
> The names I remember are seldom the same
> As those that belong with the faces.
>
> — *Author unknown*

We've all had the experience of recognizing a face but not being able to put a name with it. Now you know why — the brain finds it easier to record images than words. Because words alone don't make a strong mental impression, some memory courses advocate associating names with an image. That can work if it's an easy name, but if it's a difficult one, I've missed half the conversation while trying to come up with an appropriate picture.

I personally don't use this technique to learn names. However, it does help to imagine a person's name written across the forehead so that name and visual image are recorded together.

In remembering names, I believe concentration and repetition work best. Here's a 3 step process to help you remember names:

1. GET THE NAME RIGHT when you first hear it. Ask it to be repeated or spelled. Study the face as you speak the name so they go into memory bank together. Readily admit when you forget and ask again. Of course, some people simply refuse to admit when they've made a mistake...

A man approached Fred Astaire as he was leaving a restaurant in Hollywood.

"How are you, Charley?" he said to Astaire. "I see you've lost some weight and you look taller too."

"I'm afraid you've made a mistake," said the famous dancer. "My name's not Charley. I'm Fred Astaire."

"Ah," the man sneered, "so you've changed your name too."

2. USE THE NAME REPEATEDLY. Say it aloud and silently. The more you use the name when you first hear it, the more of an impression it will make. One couple on a ship had an excellent suggestion for helping others remember their names. They repeatedly called or referred to each other by name for the benefit of their new acquaintances.

3. ASSOCIATE the name with someone you know. We've all done this. At the time you probably said something like, "That's my mother's name. I'll remember that." You are linking it to an established neuronal network.

Another good association technique is to link the first letter of the person's name with some cogent information about that individual. If you meet someone named Ann, for instance, and she likes to exercise, you might think of her as Athletic Ann.

You can train yourself to remember names if you really want to. Most forgetting is not the result of a poor memory, but lack of desire to remember in the first place. You may not realize it, but when you tell a person, "I'm terrible with names. I'll never remember yours," you are saying that they are not important enough for you to put the effort into remembering their name. In addition, it reinforces a poor memory concept in your subconscious.

* * * * * *

Some forgetfulness is normal at all ages. Our brains collect a lot of information over the years and sometimes it takes a while to sift through it all. Next time a word doesn't immediately spring to mind, be patient. What we call forgetfulness is often just slower reaction time. Make life easier on yourself, give your memory a little help. Don't hesitate to use memory aids.

MEMORY AIDS

Write it down. Use lists to prevent short-term memory overload.
Carry a small dictation machine.
Send yourself voice mail or email.
Use rhyme and alliteration to link items.

MEMORY BUILDING EXERCISES

1. REPETITION. Memorize a poem or song. Listen to it repeatedly. Write it down. Learn a line or two at a time. This will improve powers of concentration as well as memory.

2. ASSOCIATION: Choose four unrelated words and try to make one sentence out of them. Try it with pool, brain, chair, stoplight.

3. VISUALIZATION. Take mental snapshots. Look at a scene or object, study it, then turn away and describe it.

4. STORIES. Choose 7 - 10 unrelated words and make a mini-story.

HEALTHY BRAINS and MEMORIES Although pharmaceutical tests are constantly reporting different results, Vitamins C and E have been documented in reducing the risk of Alzheimer's Disease. Other research has found the following to be beneficial to brain and memory: Lecithin, Vitamin B1, B complex, manganese, folic acid, serotonin, fish oil, lipoid acid, acetyl L-carnitine.

Dr. Dhara Singh Khalsa, creator of "The Better Memory Kit," also recommends: CoenzymeQ10 for brain cell energy production which decreases with age. It's also depleted by statin drugs. Phosphatidyl serine has been successful in reversing memory loss.

DHA omega 3 oils. Talk to a doctor or nutritionist to determine what supplements are best for you.

SUGGESTED READING:

The Memory Workbook: Breakthrough Techniques to Exercise Your Brain and Improve Your Memory by Douglas J. Mason, Michael Lee Kohn, Karen A. Clark

QUOTES TO LIVE BY:

> *Tell me and I'll forget; show me and I may remember;*
> *involve me and I'll understand.*
> — *Chinese proverb*

MEMORY BOOSTERS

Get enough sleep. Eat right. Drink water. Exercise. Breathe deeply.

Clear your mind. Concentrate. Be interested. Pay attention.

Slight discomfort increases attention and alertness.

When attention lags, take a catnap.

Organized information is four times easier to learn and remember than random.

Move your eyes from side-to-side for about 30 seconds to activate the connections between both hemispheres of the brain and improve memory.

Count backwards from 100 to 1. Count from 1 to 100 in 3s, 4s, 6s, 7s, 8s, 9s. Count backwards from 100 in 3s, 4s, 6s etc.

Use your senses, emotions and humor to increase pathways into the brain and strengthen neural patterns.

Say what you want to remember aloud. Speak aloud when you put something down. Your voice will mark the spot.

A positive attitude improves memory and cognitive functions.

And here's a surprise — chew gum! Research discovered that chewing makes the heart beat faster which increases oxygen and glucose in the brain. Memory improved by 15% and reading speed increased up to 15% in gum chewers. Teachers are going to hate it when this news gets out!

Chapter 24

CREATIVITY

Thank goodness I was never sent to school; it would have rubbed off some of the originality.

Beatrix Potter

We don't need to be great artists be creative. Creativity is the ability to see common things in an uncommon way, think outside the box, innovate. The creative mind loves challenge, is willing to explore and experiment. Happy people are creators. They believe they have the power to make things happen and can shape their lives. They don't let obstacles stand in their way.

A man entered his study to find his 3 year old daughter typing on his word processor.

"What are you doing?" he asked.

"I'm writing a story," she replied.

"Oh," he said, "what's it about?"

"I don't know," she said, "I can't read." She didn't let that stop her! Creative people are like that. They have the courage to try something new, take risks, be different. They're not hog tied by perfectionism. Fear of failure, being wrong, making a mistake stops most people in their tracks.

It is not because things are difficult that we do not dare; it is because we do not dare that they are difficult.
— *North American Indian Seneca*

In the early years of life, before the left brain is fully developed, children are right brain oriented. Consequently, almost all children rank high in creativity before entering school. Have you ever witnessed pre-schoolers being asked a question? They jump up and down, waving their hands wildly. They desperately want to be called upon — even if they don't know the answer. They'll make one up! By second grade, children start holding back — even if they do know the answer. Fear of being wrong stifles thinking, action and creativity.

Our doubts are traitors and make us lose the good we oft might win by fearing to attempt.
— *William Shakespeare*

Since our education system emphasizes left brain skills, only 10% of 7 years olds continue to rank high in creativity. As adults, just 2% of the population is considered creative. Ironically, about 50% of adults think they're creative. Most likely they base that opinion on having certain artistic abilities rather than creative thinking and living.

Unfortunately, education is largely about learning what other people think. It's not about learning how to think. As adults, we tend to echo what we learned. The majority of people go through life with the same religion and political affiliation as their parents. We tend to adopt the same beliefs and values and prejudices of our family or culture without ever thinking about them. Being subject to the law of inertia, the brain runs the same thoughts over and over like a broken record. Behavior becomes automatic and unconscious; reactions conditioned and habitual. We fall asleep at the wheel.

To be creative, we have to break through the walls we've built around ourselves. We have to venture into the unknown, think a new thought, do something different. In short, we have to wake up. We need to wake up our brains and bodies and senses. To be creative is to be fully, vitally, enthusiastically alive. The creative mind sees the world in Technicolor. Creative living leads us in different and exciting directions. Creative people invent or discover because they use the neural network less traveled.

To bring the zest and fulfillment of creativity to our lives, we need to stop, look again, think again, ask questions. If you look at a familiar object long enough, it will suddenly seem strange, and appear in a whole new light. When Isaac Newton was asked how he discovered the law of gravity, he replied, "By thinking about it all the time." Obviously, he wasn't thinking the same thoughts over and over and over.

Make room in your mind to think about something new, to think something different. Most of our thinking today is a tired rerun of all our yesterdays. We need to get rid of some of those dusty old thoughts and make room for new ones. Most of us are suffering severe cases of mind clutter. Living in the Information Age, we tend to confuse information with intelligence. In some cases, the opposite is actually true. Remember the last time you went to one of those restaurants with menus that read like a novelette? Too much information results in muddled thinking and wrong decisions.

Because our society emphasizes rational, left brain thinking, the right, creative, imaginative hemisphere of the brain isn't getting much of a workout. Over-reliance on the analytical left brain inhibits creativity.

We suppress creative impulses. Flashes of intuitive knowledge are ignored. Years ago when I first moved to Florida, I often rode my bike to work. I kept it in the garage of my apartment building.

It was open to the outdoors, but I locked it in a bike rack. One evening upon my return from my work, I walked into the garage, past the bike rack and into the building. I was half way to the elevator before I realized what I was doing. I had the urge to keep going, take the bike upstairs, but shook my head, turned around, went back into the garage and locked my bike in the rack. The next morning it was gone.

You've no doubt had similar experiences. How many times have you heard people say, "I should have stayed with my first answer." We all have intuition or a sixth sense. If our ancestors hadn't had it, they probably wouldn't have survived. But in our relatively safe environment, we rely on our instincts and intuition much less than primitive man did. We trust the head more than the heart, and often repress our creative urges.

For almost 6 years, my husband and I lived and traveled fulltime in a large motor home. As we criss-crossed the United States and Canada, we met many people who said, "Oh, I'd love to do that but my spouse won't give up the house, leave the grandchildren, the church, the clubs…" or some such thing. No matter how alluring a change might sound, many people won't move out of their comfort zone, won't forsake the known for the unknown.

I'm not telling you to sell everything and make a major lifestyle change. However, when people get stuck in a rut and stop growing, life sometimes forces change upon them. In such cases, the change may come in the form of chaos — a sudden, unexpected upheaval. In science, chaos is the term applied to a system that has become over-full. The boundaries can no longer contain it and the system falls into disorder and confusion. But then, out of the chaos, a new, higher order emerges.

This is the process of creativity. It's both destructive and constructive. Old patterns have to fall apart before new ones can take root. We are forced out of structured, rigid thinking, complacent lifestyles. Confusion reigns for a while. But then we emerge into a new, higher, expanded state. The way to avoid chaos is to willingly and consciously stretch our parameters, enter and explore the unknown, discover who we are outside the box we built. This doesn't happen overnight. There are still periods of confusion. Sometimes we feel like we're in no man's land, treading water between the shores of the known and unknown.

> *Man can learn nothing except by going*
> *from the known to the unknown.*
> — *Claude Bernard*

The hardest part, I think, is giving up the old before the new has emerged. There is an empty space, a void. Feelings of guilt or fear or sadness arise when we come face to face with these empty spaces in ourselves and our lives. The tendency is to rush to fill the void. The word avoid means to evade, stay away from. Most people avoid the void at any cost. We equate nothingness and death, but the void is in fact the matrix of creativity. Out of it new ideas and possibilities arise. The higher form emerges. We need to sink into and experience the void, and stay with it. It is the fertile soil of the soul. From it rises the phoenix, the new life.

Creative living is challenging and exciting if not always comfortable. It's a process of re-creation often resulting in you being different from the you you used to be. Do you find that exciting or scary?

"The real shock when I stopped working was that I had to start thinking," said one retiree. "When I was working, everything followed a set routine. I knew what I had to do each day and it was like being on automatic pilot. With retirement, I had to stop and look at my life, at myself, what I wanted. I had to make decisions. It was scary. But the hardest part of it was long periods of time in which I didn't have anything to do. I couldn't just relax. I felt guilty."

I lived in solitude in the country and noticed how the monotony of a quiet life stimulates the creative mind.

— *Albert Einstein*

We could develop creativity simply by questioning everything: Is there another to look at this? Is there another way to think about this? Is there another way to do this? That's how scientists create. They probe, and question and look at things from different angles. Jonas Salk's creative method eventually led to the polio vaccine. He said, "I developed a way to examine my experiences by imagining myself as the object in which I was interested. ...I used this system to imagine myself as a virus or a cancer cell to sense what it would be like. I would also imagine myself as the immune system to reconstruct what I would do in combat with a virus or cancer cell. ...I would then know which questions to ask next. ...I could solve problems more easily because I could look at them simultaneously from the viewpoints of subject and object. It was like I had been looking at everything through one pair of glasses and now I had a new pair that was showing me things I hadn't seen before. A lot of my opinions and judgments gradually slipped away."

Creative thinking and living is essential to stimulating the brain, building dendrites and growing. It makes you an interested and interesting person. While a creative approach to life may inspire an alteration in your external life, the real change is internal. On the surface, nothing may change but you feel more alive, more open, more present. You're willing to take chances, experiment. You might decide to put a square peg in a round hole. You know that sometimes you have to put things where they don't fit for the moment because in so doing, you open up a whole new, wonderful array of possibilities.

You will do foolish things but do them with enthusiasm.

— *Colette*

Creativity is a way of life more than an artistic undertaking, but don't be surprised if living a more creative life leads you into artistic avenues. One thing you can be sure of, developing a creative approach to life will make your days more fun. The seeds of the child's creative mind are still within us and we can re-awaken wonder and curiosity. We just need to give ourselves permission to venture into the unknown, take risks, possibly fail, but stretch beyond our pre-set limits. A friend of mine had the courage to do this.

ANN'S STORY

My children are grown, and I have to say that my grandchildren are the best part of my life. But I knew after age 50 (I'm 61 now) that I needed to find what "Ann" needed to do to express herself as a real person. I discovered a creative self deep within that I didn't even know existed.

I took a few photographic courses at The Disney Institute which doesn't exist any longer. I tapped into an ability inside me and I think that was the jumping off place for me. After my photographs had been developed and returned to me in class, I looked at them and said to myself, "These are really good." It was interesting, I didn't need anyone else to tell me. I knew right then that I had an ability to express myself through film. Not long after that, I started a photographic card business. That was about five years ago.

For me the card business isn't about money. I'm lucky if it pays for developing and card stock. To me, it's about expressing myself and giving to others. I'll tell you one story that happened recently. A dear friend sent one of my sunrise over the ocean cards to a friend whose husband died in his sleep last week. The bereaved widow immediately called my friend and said, "You will never know how special your card and note were to me. For days I've asked God to send me a sign that Ted is okay. When I opened your card, I knew my prayer was answered. You see, Ted wanted his ashes strewn at sea, and the picture was confirmation for me that he is all right."

The fact that I can touch people I don't even know gives me a sense of grace. One of the best parts is that I give myself the approval I need; I don't wait for anyone else to do it for me.

Recently a painting course was offered at a club I belong to. I thought about it and went through the mental gymnastics of fear, childhood experiences of not being successful in art class, maybe I'll look inept, what if I can't do it. But then I decided to take a step into the unknown, out of my comfort zone, and I signed up for the painting class. Am I the best in the class, you ask? Probably the worst, but those 2½ hours of my time are the best. An interesting side benefit is that I don't look at things the same way since I became involved in photography and painting.

Sometimes I feel a little like Peter Pan: I'll never grow up. But maybe I have. I guess I would have to say life is about growing, no matter what the age. So what if you fail? Try something else until you find what interests you, what you really enjoy. I love to encourage others to try new things. Some are open and willing, others are closed and fearful. They miss so much. I don't want to be on my death bed and say, "I wish I had _____, and now it's too late."

THE CREATIVE APPROACH

1. BE CURIOUS. Read interesting material. Watch educational programs. Entertain new, different and foreign ideas. Ask what if, why not and how can questions. Probe. Learn how things work. Study people. What makes them tick? Try something you've never done before. Study something outside your usual areas of interest.

> *A sense of curiosity is nature's original school of education.*
> — *Smiley Blanton*

2. BE ADVENTUROUS. Explore, experiment. Go places you've never been before. Take a different route to work, the post office or the store. Try different ways of doing things. Explore people's minds. What do they think and why? How did they reach their conclusions?

Make changes. Just changing your style of dress can spark new feelings and ideas. Make each day a different color day. How do various colors make you feel, affect your mood? Wear something radically different from your usual style.

> *Twenty years from now you will be more disappointed by the things that you didn't do than by the ones you did do. So throw off the bowlines. Sail away from the safe harbor. Catch the trade winds in your sails.*
> *Explore. Dream. Discover.*
> — *Mark Twain*

3. BE WILLING TO BE WRONG. Where would scientists be if they were afraid of failure? Nothing grabs attention like failure. Errors are learning devices. They point us in the right direction. Thomas Alva Edison said, "I have not failed. I've just found 10,000 ways that won't work."

> *A man's errors are his portals of discovery.*
> — *James Joyce*

Think of something you once considered a big failure. What good came out of that? What did you learn? Find out what's wrong with an idea but also what's worth building on. If we're not making any mistakes, we must simply be repeating what we already know. Take some creative risks and don't be concerned with results.

4. OBSERVE. Many of the memory skills are necessary to creativity: observation, attention to detail, making associations, creating images and stories. Comedians are observation artists. They notice the little idiosyncrasies in life and create humor.

> *To acquire knowledge, one must study, but to acquire wisdom, one must observe.*
> — *Marilyn vos Savant*

5. USE YOUR IMAGINATION. Throw logic out the window and let your imagination run away with you. Write a poem, draw a picture, make up a story. Read fiction to stimulate imagination. Stop at crises points and ask yourself what you would do. How would you resolve the dilemma, the conflict? Pretend you are teaching a disabled person how to walk. How would you describe balance, motion, coordination etc.? How would you describe colors to a blind person, sounds to a deaf person? What feelings do different colors stimulate? Imagine that a problem or an illness could talk. What would it tell you?

> *Imagination is more important than knowledge.*
> — *Einstein*

6. CHANGE YOUR PERSPECTIVE. Go beyond established thinking. Pretend you're in a debate. Take a stand against your strongly held beliefs. Challenge your basic assumptions and shatter the prevailing mindset. Let go of judgments and rules. Change established ways of doing things. Brain storm. How many different ways can you tackle a problem? Don't stop with the first solution.

Doubt what others take for granted. Look at a situation and say: It's not what everyone thinks it is. Things are not as they appear. Give a different interpretation. Say, "this is not a problem, but an opportunity in disguise."

There is no truth. There is only perception.
— *Gustave Flaubert*

Creating an analogy or metaphor to describe a problem provides new insight. Picture a goal and then work backwards through the steps that would get you to the goal. Open a favorite inspirational book, run your finger down the page and read a few lines. Can it help you perceive a situation in a different way?

7. HAVE FUN. A fun environment and a playful, silly attitude ignites creativity. Humor is mind expanding, sparks new perceptions and ideas. It stretches thinking, forces us to combine ideas not usually associated with each other. Do something silly and fun at least once a week — go to an amusement park, build sand castles, watch a funny movie.

Remember these two things: play hard and have fun.
— *Tony Gwynn*

✳ ✳ ✳ ✳ ✳ ✳

Creative thinking awakens intuition; they function in tandem. Intuition comes to us as a feeling. We explain certain actions and decisions by saying, "I don't know why I did that. I just had a feeling." Pay attention to those feelings. Notice when you're energetically pulled toward or away from something. Listen to instincts and not just intellect. If you haven't used intuition for a long time, that can be a little scary. It may suggest something ambiguous or contrary to what you think is logical. Learn to trust it. In one study of thousands of business executives, 80% credited their success to relying on intuition.

SUGGESTED READING:
Cracking Creativity: The Secrets of Creative Genius
by Michael Michalko

Blink by Matthew Gladwell

MORE INFORMATION: www.jpb.com/creative/creative.php; www.creativityforlife.com

QUOTES TO LIVE BY:

When in doubt, make a fool of yourself. There is a microscopically Thin line between being brilliantly creative and acting like the most Gigantic idiot on earth. So what the hell, leap.

— *Cynthia Heimel*

Chapter 25

THE POWER OF LAUGHTER

*Humor is the great thing,
the saving thing.*

*The minute it crops up,
all our irritation*

*And resentments slip away,
and a Sunny spirit takes their
place.*

Mark Twain

WHAT IF...

You could improve your health?
And your mind?
And your mood?

WHAT IF...

You didn't need anything outside yourself to do it?
You could do it right now?
You could do it any time, any place?

GREAT NEWS: You can! The evidence is in and growing by the day...

LAUGHTER IS GOOD FOR YOU! IT...

Produces endorphins that counter stress
Boosts the immune system
Relieves pain
Increases blood flow
Stimulates the brain
Aids memory
Improves mood

Raises self-confidence
Transcends logic and negative thinking
Overcomes feelings of fear, isolation, depression, anger
Creates a bond between people
Expands awareness and perception.

LAUGHTER MAKES US FEEL BETTER PHYSICALLY, MENTALLY AND EMOTIONALLY!

Wow! That's powerful! If laughter can do all that, why aren't we doing more of it? Ironically, in this day and age when we have scientific proof of the power of laughter, we are laughing less than our grandparents' generation. One hundred years ago, adults laughed 3 times more than we do today. Children laugh 300 - 400 times a day compared to an adult's measly 10 - 18. Fortunately, we can change these numbers. Humor is all around us. We just need to re-train ourselves to see it. We'll talk more about that in coming chapters, but first let's take a closer look at the benefits of laughter.

LAUGHTER and HEALTH

A good laugh and a long sleep are the best cures in the doctor's book.
— *Irish Proverb*

In 1983, Norman Cousins described his astonishing recovery from a debilitating disease in Anatomy Of An Illness. He credited his recovery in large measure to humor. I believe that book played a significant role in alerting the medical profession to the affect of emotions and laughter on health and healing. Since its publication, a great deal of research has revealed why laughter is virtually a miracle drug.

Laughter stimulates the immune system. Tests were done on people before and after watching sitcoms for 30 - 60 minutes. Results showed an increase in immune system activity raising its ability to prevent and combat colds, flu and sinus problems. Another clinical study concluded: "…it's clear that there is something about humor and laughter that causes the immune system to 'turn on'.….and do more effectively what it is designed to do — promote health and wellness…"

> *Warning: Humor may be hazardous to your illness.*
> — *Ellie Katz*

Laughter gives the heart a workout and helps lower the risk of heart disease and stroke. It increases cardiovascular flexibility, raises heart rate and lowers blood pressure. At the same time laughter, like deep breathing, increases circulation and the flow of oxygen and nutrients to the tissues. Stress decreases blood flow about 35% but laughter increases it by 22%.

BULLETIN: LAUGHING CAN KEEP YOU ALIVE! If you or someone near you has a heart attack, simulating a hearty laugh (Ha! Ha! Ha!) or coughing every few seconds stimulates heart and chest muscles like CPR does and can keep your heart functioning until medics arrive. Doctors also advise most people to promptly chew an aspirin if they think they're having a heart attack.

Laughter reduces pain. Research has shown that laughter relaxes muscles, produces anti-inflammatory agents and triggers the release of endorphins, the body's natural painkillers. Patients exposed to laughter after surgery or prior to painful therapy experience less pain. *In Anatomy Of An Illness*, Norman Cousins writes, "I made the joyous discovery that ten minutes of genuine belly laughter had an anesthetic effect and would give me at least two hours of pain free sleep."

Hormones released by stress suppress the immune system and constrict blood vessels. Laughter is a stress buster. It strengthens the immune system, relaxes muscles and increases endorphins which counter pain. It also stimulates the production of serotonin sparking feelings of well-being. Laughter acts as an internal roto-router, shaking up the insides, relaxing muscles and releasing tension. It massages internal organs, works the respiratory system and builds abdominal and back muscles. Research by Dr. William Fry of Stanford University led him to conclude that…

100 LAUGHS = 10 minutes of aerobic exercise.

All this good news about laughter has given rise to humor therapists and laugh clubs all over the world. Since laughter is contagious, and the body can't tell the difference between real and simulated laughter, the clubs usually start with deep breathing and loud chants of ho ho ho and ha ha ha. Soon everyone is genuinely laughing. Some in the medical community have even prescribed laughter. A Pittsburgh hospital provides a 24 hour television channel called *Humor Helps Healing*. They know…

LAUGHTER IS THE BEST MEDICINE.

LAUGHTER and HAPPINESS

If it were not for these stories, jokes, jests, I should die; they give vent − are the vents − of my moods and gloom.
— Abraham Lincoln

Laughter is a natural anti-depressant. Many comedians discovered early in life that humor is an escape route from pain. George Lopez, a comedian who now has his own sitcom, never knew his father, was abandoned by his mother and raised by a cold, angry grandmother. Of his childhood, he said, "I never smiled because no one made me feel like I was alive." Enthusiastic response to his humor gave him a sense of acceptance and love he had never experienced.

With humor, we can also alleviate other people's pain. As a child, Jim Carrey slept in his tap shoes in case he needed to cheer up his chronically ill mother and manic depressive father during the night. After her mother and father divorced, Ellen DeGeneres discovered she had the amazing ability to turn her mother's tears to laughter.

Nothing dispels negative feelings faster than a good laugh. It provides a cathartic release of emotional tension. It undoes harmful biochemical changes. If we can sustain the positive emotions laughter elicits, we can overcome feelings of isolation and depression.

Following one my laughter lectures, a gentleman told me that he was drowning in grief after his wife died. He was watching television one day and something made him laugh — really laugh out loud. Immediately, he noticed that he felt better, the best he'd felt in months. Thereafter, he embarked on his own healing through humor. He started focusing on all the good times and humorous experiences he and his wife had shared. He found himself smiling and laughing again. The more he laughed, the more his burden of sorrow eased. Gradually, his entire mood and outlook on life shifted.

> *Laughter is the sun that drives winter from the human face.*
> — *Victor Hugo*

Laughter can help us rise above the situation we are in and broaden our outlook. Carol Burnett said "humor is tragedy plus time." Why? Because time lessens our mental, emotional involvement, enabling us to see things from a different perspective. Have you not said in the midst of a seeming catastrophe, "We're going to look back on this and laugh." Humor can increase cope-ability by giving us that same sense of detachment and altered perception in the moment.

> *Laughter gives us distance. It allows us to*
> *step back from an event, deal with it and then move on.*
> — *Bob Newhart*

When we can find humor in circumstances, we experience a sense of power over them and that immediately alleviates stress. Laughter activates joyful, hopeful feelings, revitalizes people and eases worry. Seeing the humor in life, laughing more, is the fastest, easiest way to change one's perspective and experience. That's why a good laugh is an express train out of anger.

Remember the Law of the Vacuum? Opposites cannot occupy the same space at the same time. It is simply impossible to laugh and be angry simultaneously. Friends and families often have their inside jokes, and a shared punch line can break through discord. Like the one in this story…

One day a lion in the jungle was feeling particularly full of himself. He strutted about demanding that other animals pay homage to him. He went up to a pack of hyenas and roared, "Who is the King of the Jungle?"

The hyenas bowed down and cried, "You are, your Majesty! You are the King of the Jungle."

He went on his way and spotted a giraffe. He walked up to him and demanded, "Giraffe! Who is the King of the Jungle?"

The giraffe lowered his long neck and said, "You are, your Royal Highness. You are the King of the Jungle."

Next the lion spotted an elephant napping by a pond. He awakened the elephant with a mighty roar and demanded, "Elephant! Tell me, who is the King of the Jungle?"

The elephant lumbered to his feet, took the lion in his mighty trunk and slammed him repeatedly against a tree. Then he dropped him, stomped on him and kicked him into the pond.

The lion, all battered and bruised, dragged himself from the pond, looked at the elephant and said, "Just because you don't know the answer, you don't have to get mad."

My husband and I have thrown that line at the other in the midst of conflict, and immediately we both crack up. Without the hostility that had been building, we are better able to calmly and rationally discuss the issue at hand.

Laughter is the shortest distance between two people.
— *Victor Borge*

Laughter dispels negativity. It diminishes aggression and creates harmony between people. Laughter like happiness is contagious; it lifts everyone's spirits. A sense of humor usually ranks higher than intellect and looks on tests that determine what a woman is seeking in a mate.

Whether we're laughing or making someone else laugh, we feel better. And when we feel good, we make better decisions.

LAUGHTER and THE BRAIN

The kind of humor I like is the thing that makes me laugh for five seconds and think for ten minutes.
— *William Davis*

Humor is mentally nutritious. It produces serotonin and endorphins which increase the ability of neurons to communicate. It engages both hemispheres of the brain which increases awareness, thinking and understanding. The detachment and expanded perspective provided by humor are skills necessary for problem solving.

Humor releases tension and stabilizes mood which enables us to concentrate and absorb more. Humor increases learning and memory. Often a story is involved and, as you know, we visualize and remember stories better than isolated facts. To grasp humor, we have to pay attention to details which means we take in more information. We are more likely to remember something that involves humor.

Comedy promotes good feelings and open mindedness. Humor can be used to persuade, entertain, resolve arguments and unite people. It broadens understanding and ignites imagination. It makes us go beyond the expected, and shift perception. Often we have to make a quick mental leap to get the joke, as in this one…

> It was high school graduation day in a small, backwoods town. The principal proudly announced that more seniors were graduating this year than ever before.
>
> "For a while," he said, "it looked like every last senior was going to graduate, but unfortunately Billy J. failed his final math test and will not be graduating."
>
> Hearing this, Billy's classmates groaned, then jumped to their feet and cried, "One more chance, one more chance!"
>
> The principal laughed, "Oh, what the heck! Billy, come on up here. Your classmates want you to have one more chance and I'm gonna give it to you. Now think real hard. How much is 8 times 6?"
>
> Billy closed his eyes, furrowed his brow, finally looked up and said hesitantly, "48?" Whereupon his classmates jumped to their feet and yelled, "One more chance! One more chance!"

What a powerful, natural healer we have in laughter. People who laugh easily are healthier, happier and more resilient. Laughter can lift emotions, dispel negativity and depression, strengthen the immune system, release stress and improve mind and memory. So, I urge you to laugh loud, laugh long and laugh often.

SUGGESTED READING:

Anatomy of an Illness by Norman Cousins

QUOTES TO LIVE BY:

> *Humor has a way of bringing people together. It unites people*
> *In fact, I'm rather serious when I suggest that someone should*
> *plant a few whoopee cushions in the United Nations.*
>
> — *Ron Dentinger*

Chapter 26

DEVELOPING YOUR COMEDIC ABILITY

When I told my friends I was going to be a comedian, they laughed at me

Author Unknown

Laughter is triggered when we find something humorous. At different ages and stages of life, different types of humor appeal to us. So the essential question to ask yourself before trying to be a comedian: Who is my audience?

Very young children like jokes and riddles that are quick, simple and easy to grasp. The sillier, the better. Think back to some of your favorites when you were a child. Why did the chicken cross the road? Why did the man throw the clock out the window? The same funny story, movie or joke doesn't cease to tickle children. They love it to be repeated over and over, and laugh louder each time.

From an early age through adolescence, fascination with bodies makes what's known as bathroom or toilet humor a favorite. Particularly among the boys. Adolescents like to express their rebelliousness with gross jokes. They also find other people's mistakes, misfortunes and shortcomings funny. It helps them mask their insecurities and feel superior.

As we mature and build self-esteem, we may still laugh at other's misfortunes, but now it is usually out of a sense of relief — thank goodness that isn't me. Our sense of humor develops as we age. It often becomes more intellectual and subtle.

To be appreciated by the most people, the core of humor must be general, related to experiences we can all identify with — life's every day problems, stresses, universal issues. Subjects like the relationship between the sexes...

Love is blind, but marriage is a real eye-opener.

In our marriage we agreed to never go to bed angry. We're exhausted! Haven't been to bed all week.

Marriage counselor: Do you enjoy talking to each other?

Wife: Yes, we do. The problem is listening to each other.

There is always the risk that what one person thinks amusing, another may find offensive. What men and women think funny can vary considerably. Don't be surprised if the joke your pals loved goes over like a lead balloon with the opposite sex. Always try to be aware of your audience.

A good joke can fall flat in the wrong hands — or mouth. There are elements to telling jokes and expressing humor that when adhered to can make even dull stories funny.

1. INCONGRUITY is central to humor. We follow a story anticipating one outcome and a sudden twist leads to something different, illogical, unexpected. When expectations get turned on their head and something completely unanticipated occurs, we find the incompatibility and surprise funny.

A playwright took a friend to a party. She sat down in a wicker chair, the wicker gave way and she jackknifed through it. The shocked hush that fell over the partygoers was broken when the playwright said, "Beatrice, how many times have I told you that isn't funny."

When we hear this story, our minds lead us in one direction and we anticipate a specific outcome. We expect concern and sympathy. The totally unexpected and incongruous response of the playwright makes us laugh.

2. RELEASE. Laughter relieves tension. When we get emotionally involved in a story or joke, we build emotional tension. Humor opens a valve, pent up energy escapes, and we instantly feel relieved. That's why humor improves the ability to handle stress. The release relaxes the body and opens the mind.

In the previous story, we can picture poor Beatrice falling through the chair and feel stressed for her. The laughter provides relief. **The build up of tension followed by sudden release is the formula most jokes are built around.**

3. RHYTHM. A good story teller has rhythm and timing— and so does a good joke. **95% of jokes have a three step rhythmic build up.** Something happens three times or in three different ways or the same words are repeated three times. Tension builds. Then comes the punch line, the unexpected twist, and with it a sudden release of the tension.

All the elements of humor are present in this joke:

A man was approaching a bar when he heard a voice say, "Hey, Mister." He looked around, didn't see anyone, headed for the door but heard the voice again, "Hey, Mister." He stopped, surveyed the area and shook his head in bewilderment when the voice spoke again, "Mister! Down here." He looked down and saw a dog looking up at him.

"It's me talking to you," the dog said. The man looked at the dog in astonishment, closed his eyes, shook his head. "Don't worry," said the dog. "You're not going crazy. I can really talk. Now, how would you like to make some quick money? Take me into the bar with you and bet everyone that I can talk. We'll split the winnings."

When the man regained his composure, he readily agreed. He walked into the bar with the dog and bet everyone there that the dog could talk. When all the money, was on the bar, he turned to the dog and said, "Speak."

The dog looked at him and wagged his tail. "Speak!" the man commanded. The dog twisted his head as if trying to understand. Growing desperate, the man yelled, "Speak, Speak! Say something!"

The dog merely sat down on the floor. The people in the bar burst into laughter. The man signed a pile of IOUs and, head hanging, walked out of the bar with the dog.

"You rotten, no good dog," he said when they were outside. "Do you have any idea how much money I just lost? It will take me a year to pay it off. You've ruined me…"

"Relax, relax," said the dog. "Think about it. Tomorrow we'll get 5 to 1!"

This has all the elements of a good joke for all audiences. The material is totally inoffensive. There is immediate humor in the illogical image of a talking dog. The rhythmic build up is in asking the dog to speak three different times. We get emotionally involved. I'm sure we can all sympathize with the man putting himself on the line, betting money he couldn't afford to lose and then being humiliated. We grow tense with him. Then comes the unexpected twist, the laughter, the release of tension, the relief.

No matter what age we may be, we can nurture a sense of humor and develop comedic talents. Pay attention to what makes you laugh — a certain comic, television show, reading funny material, playing with children? Whatever it is, do more of it. Cultivate a playful attitude. See the silliness and humor in daily life. Practice telling jokes and making others laugh.

Laughter is contagious. Start laughing and other people soon join in. Spend time with funny people. You'll start to think like them. On one cruise ship, we had a table mate who was a master of puns. Hardly a sentence could be spoken without Pat making a humorous pun. One evening he left his eyeglasses on the table. The waiter called after him, "Excuse me, sir. You've forgotten your glasses."

"Oh, my," said Pat. "I've made a spectacle of myself." By the end of the cruise, every person at our table was a punster.

Develop your wit. Study George Carlin's brilliant commentaries on the contradictions, incongruities and absurdities of life...

Why do overlook and oversee mean opposite things?

Why do they put pictures of criminals up in the Post Office? Why don't they just put their pictures on the postage stamps so the mailmen can look for them while they deliver the mail?

Does pushing the elevator button more than once make it arrive faster? Studying the witty remarks of others can help you think that way...

Bob Hope: There are nearly 60 golf courses in the Palm Springs area and Jerry Ford never knows which one he'll play until he hits his first drive.

After playing a round of golf with Arnold Palmer, Frank Sinatra asked him, "What do you think of my game?" "Not bad," said Palmer "but I still prefer golf."

Laugh at yourself. Self-deprecating humor says you don't take yourself too seriously and puts others at ease. Henny Youngman and Rodney Dangerfield were masters of this type of humor...

Henny Youngman: I was so ugly when I was born, the doctor slapped my mother.

Rodney Dangerfield: A girl phoned me and said, "Come on over, there's nobody home." I went over. She was right. There was nobody home.

Rodney Dangerfield: I asked my Dad if I could go ice skating. He said, "Wait until it gets warmer."

Stretch your imagination and wit by re-working common idioms. Take the beginning of a cliché and add your own ending.

If at first you don't succeed _____

A stitch in time _____

If it's worth doing _____

Here are some answers from 1st graders....

Don't bite the hand that — looks dirty.
A penny saved is — not much.
When the blind lead the blind — get out of the way.
A miss is as good as — a mister.

With stress the #1 cause of illness, and depression on its way to epidemic proportions, we can't afford not to laugh. Laughter is an easy, fun way to improve health, elevate mood, improve performance, increase cope-ability and enhance relationships. It's a muscle that gets stronger with use, and a miracle drug with no bad side effects.

Laughter can light up your life!

SUGGESTED READING:
What's So Funny? How To Sharpen Your Sense Of Humor
by Paul Moran

MORE INFORMATION: There are countless joke sites on the internet.

QUOTES TO LIVE BY:

> *The most wasted of all days is that on which one has not laughed.*
>
> *— Nicolas Chamfort*

Chapter 27

LAUGH BOOK

We don't laugh cause we're happy;
we're happy because we laugh.

William James

If your days are naturally filled with laughter, good for you! But if like most adults, you aren't laughing enough, start looking for humor. When you find it, write it down. Keep a Laugh Book. That's a notebook full of funny stories, jokes, humorous experiences and happy quotes — things that at the very least bring a smile to your face. Add to it every day. And, if you don't find anything to laugh about some days, read what you've already recorded. You'll soon be laughing again. Your Laugh Book will also provide material to entertain others.

A laugh is a smile that bursts.
— Mary H. Waldrip

Once you open your eyes and ears to humor, you will find it everywhere. Here are a few potential sources:

Television	T-shirts and bumper stickers
Internet	Magazines and newspapers
Books	Personal experience

Following are suggestions for categories and corresponding examples.

KIDS SAY THE FUNNIEST THINGS

I owe a great debt of gratitude to all the parents, school teachers and Sunday school teachers who share the funny and often profound things that kids say. I love to collect them, and laugh every time I reread them.

Answers to questions on tests:

Question: What is a terminal illness?
 Answer: When you're sick at the airport.

Question: What is a fibula?
 Answer: A very little lie.

Question: How can you delay milk turning sour?
 Answer: Keep it in the cow

Question: What happens to your body as you age?
 Answer: When you get old, so do your bowels and you get intercontinental.

From 6th grade essays:

Johann Bach wrote many musical compositions and had a large number of children. He practiced on an old spinster he kept in the attic.

Ancient Egypt was inhabited by mummies and they all wrote in hydraulics. They lived in the Sarah Dessert. The climate of the Sarah is such that the inhabitants have to live elsewhere.

Sir Francis Drake circumcised the world with a 100-foot clipper.

From Sunday School students:

Question: What is the 10th commandment?
  Answer: Thou shall not take the covers off the neighbor's wife.

Lot's wife was a pillar of salt by day, but a ball of fire by night. Christians have only one spouse. This is called monotony.

The seventh commandment is thou shalt not admit adultery.

KIDS SAY THE WISEST THINGS

Here are more answers children gave to the question, "What is love?"

Age 5: Love is what's in the room with you at Christmas if you stop opening presents and listen.

Age 7: Love is when you tell a guy you like his shirt, then he wears it everyday.

Age 8: When my grandmother got arthritis, she couldn't bend over and paint her toenails anymore. So my grandfather does it for her all the time, even when his hands got arthritis too. That's love.

Age 6: If you want to learn to love better, you should start with a friend whom you hate.

MIX-UPS and MISPRINTS

The way things are written or said can give unintended meaning and humor.

From newspaper headlines:

Hospital Sued By 7 Foot Doctors

Miners Refuse To Work After Death

Survivor Of Siamese Twins Join Parents

Panda Mating Fails; Veterinarian Takes Over

Enraged Cow Injures Farmer With Axe.

From classified ads:

Wanted: Boy to take care of horses who can speak German.

From church bulletins:

This being Easter Sunday, we will ask Mrs. L. to come forward and lay an egg on the altar.

The ladies of the church have cast off clothing of every kind. They can be seen in the church basement Saturday.

From letters to the Welfare Department:

I am very much annoyed to find that you have branded my son illiterate. This is a dirty lie as I was married a week before he was born.

I've been in bed with the doctor for two weeks and he doesn't do me any good. If things don't improve, I will have to send for another doctor.

Mrs. Jones has not had any clothes for a year and has been visited regularly by the clergy.

T-SHIRTS and BUMPER STICKERS

Humor is all around us. Just listen to the titles and words of some songs. Or read the bumper stickers on cars.

Real country western song titles:

I hope you're living as high on the hog as the pig you turned out to be.

If the phone doesn't ring, it's me.

She's just a name dropper, and now she's droppin' mine.

Bumper stickers:

I childproofed my house… but they still get in.

My reality check just bounced.

Life is short. Make fun of it.

JOKES

An 85 year old man went to the doctor for a complete physical.

"You're in fantastic shape," the doctor told him. "There's not a thing wrong with you."

"That's good news," said the 85 year old, "because I'm getting married next week."

"No kidding! Congratulations. And what about your wife to be? Is she in good health?"

"Oh, perfect," said the 85 year old. "She's only 25."

"25??!!" cried the doctor. "You're marrying a 25 year old?"

"Yes, is there something wrong with that?"

"No no," said the doctor. "It's just that, well, 85 and 25... You know, she should have someone closer to her age to satisfy certain needs. Let me give you a piece of advice. Take in a boarder."

A year later the man returned for his annual physical. "So, how's the marriage going?" the doctor asked.

"Wonderful," the man beamed. "My wife is pregnant."

"Really?" said the doctor with a knowing smile. "So you followed my advice and took in a boarder?"

"Oh, yes," said the man. "She's pregnant too!"

TRUE STORIES

Truth is not only stranger than fiction, it is often funnier.

Questions asked by lawyers in actual court cases:

Were you present when your picture was taken?

Was it you or your younger brother who was killed in the war?

Now Doctor, isn't it true that when a person dies in his sleep, he doesn't know about it until the next morning?

From employee evaluations:

He should go far and the sooner he starts, the better.

This employee is depriving some village of an idiot.

If you gave him a penny for his thoughts, you'd get change.

From epitaphs on tombstones:

Here lies Johnny Yeast. Pardon me for not rising.

Here lies Lester Moore. Four slugs from a .44. No Les No More.

Here lies an Atheist. All dressed up and no place to go.

From label instructions on consumer goods:

On bottle of sleep aids: Warning: May cause drowsiness.

On package of peanuts: Warning: contains nuts.

On a Swedish chain saw: Do not attempt to stop chain with your hands or genitals.

Humor is all around us. Don't miss it!

SUGGESTED READING: *Laughter, the Best Medicine: Jokes, Gags, and Laugh Lines from America's Most Popular Magazine* by Reader's Digest

MORE INFORMATION: The monthly Reader's Digest is always a good source for humor.
Also see their website: www.rd.com

If you have satellite radio, you can receive comedy channels 24 hours a day. For more information, go to www.xmradio.com

QUOTES TO LIVE BY:

A person without a sense of humor is like a wagon without springs - jolted by every pebble in the road.

— Henry Ward Beecher

Chapter 28

MAKE THE BEST OF THE REST OF YOUR LIFE

To live content with small means; to seek elegance rather than luxury,
and refinement rather than fashion; to be worthy, not respectable, and wealthy, not rich; to study hard, think quietly, talk gently, act frankly; to listen to stars and birds, to babes and sages, with open heart; to bear all cheerfully, do all bravely, await occasions, hurry never. In a word, to let the spiritual, unbidden and unconscious, grow up through the common.

This is to be my symphony.

William Henry Channing

If you've ever been on a cruise ship you know that there is a disembarkation talk at the end of every cruise. This chapter is our disembarkation talk, a chance to leave you with a few last thoughts to take with you.

Human beings have an inclination to be negative. Sadly, it's true. It's in our genes. The genes are interested in two things: survival and reproduction. To survive and win mates, one has to be stronger, smarter, slicker than his peers. Lyall Watson in his book *Dark Nature* describes what he calls three rules of the genes:

1. Be nasty to outsiders.
2. Be nice to insiders.
3. Cheat whenever possible.

Doesn't sound very nice, does it? But when you consider how difficult it was to survive in the world when human beings first appeared, those rules make sense. Outsiders are not to be trusted. They may invade our territory, steal our food, kill us. On the other hand, it behooves us to be good to insiders, those within our tribe. We need their help and support. Finally, cheating can enable us get what we want, need, feel entitled to.

As we evolved, altruism and cooperation came into the picture. They too are survival instincts. When mankind shifted from a nomadic to an agricultural, settled society, altruism and cooperation proved beneficial for survival. But these qualities were in addition to the three rules. We still fear outsiders, practice deception and are suspicious of other races, cultures and religions.

Why am I mentioning this? Because I want you to understand people's fears and inclination to be negative. I want you to know why the majority of most people's thoughts fall into the negative category. Most of all, I want you to realize you can rise above primal instincts. Beyond the genes, the body and the brain, we have a mind. All too often we function on automatic pilot, letting our genes and conditioning and fears control our lives. But mind transcends those things and has power over them.

We have instincts but we also have choice. We will never achieve our potential or find real happiness if we allow our primitive brain and genes to dictate our thoughts and behavior. With choice and commitment, we can overcome baser instincts. We have fear but we also have love. There is ugliness but there is also beauty. There is hatred but there is also kindness. There is darkness but there is also light. The choice is ours.

In the following letter written by Fra Giovanni in 1513, he urges a dear friend to see beyond the shadows…

I am your friend and my love for you goes deep. There is nothing I can give you which you have not got, but there is much, very much, that, while I cannot give it, you can take.

No heaven can come to us unless our hearts find rest in today. Take heaven!

No peace lies in the future which is not hidden in this present little instant. Take peace!

The gloom of the world is but a shadow. Behind it, yet within our reach is joy. There is radiance and glory in the darkness could we but see — and to see we have only to look. I beseech you to look!

Life is so generous a giver, but we, judging its gifts by the covering, cast them away as ugly, or heavy or hard. Remove the covering and you will find beneath it a living splendor, woven of love, by wisdom, with power.

Welcome it, grasp it, touch the angel's hand that brings it to you. Everything we call a trial, a sorrow, or a duty, believe me, that angel's hand is there, the gift is there, and the wonder of an overshadowing presence. Our joys, too, be not content with them as joys. They, too, conceal diviner gifts.

Life is so full of meaning and purpose, so full of beauty — beneath its covering — that you will find earth but cloaks your heaven.

Courage, then, to claim it, that is all. But courage you have, and the knowledge that we are all pilgrims together, wending through unknown country, home.

And so, at this time, I greet you. Not quite as the world sends greetings, but with profound esteem and with the prayer that for you now and forever, the day breaks, and the shadows flee away.

We can surrender to our genes and conditioning, our regrets and grievances or we can take responsibility for who we are, what we think and how we act. We can bemoan the injustice in the world or we can be a beacon of light in the darkness. We can separate or we can join. We can be guided by fear or by faith. We can be apathetic or enthusiastic. The choice is ours.

As you make your daily choices, remember...

Aging has changed and it's time to change our mind about aging. Don't buy into *old* attitudes or accept other people's negative beliefs about aging.

Focus of attention creates. Change your mind and you'll change your life.

It is never what is happening that upsets us. It is always what we *think* about what's happening.

Happiness is something you decide on ahead of time.

Gratitude = great attitude. Pessimism is hazardous to your health.

Growth comes from going beyond our boundaries. Courage doesn't mean going into the unknown without fear. It means going in spite of it.

Exercise is crucial to the health of body and brain.

Dendrites determine mental acuity, and they can be built at any age.

We determine what we will be in the next moment.

Consciously or unconsciously, we are always making choices.

Knowledge becomes yours when you act on it.

Interest produces concentration. Concentration produces interest.

Developing your non-dominant side and all your senses will improve brain function and memory.

Laughter has physical, mental and emotional benefits.

The greatest ally or enemy you will ever have is your own thinking.

> *To exist is to change, to change is to mature,*
> *to mature is to go on creating oneself endlessly.*
> — *Henri Bergson*

Life can be amazing, full of wonder and joy. Wonder has lost its meaning... "I wonder what we'll have for dinner. I wonder what time it is." True wonder is a sense of amazement and an aspect of joy. Children have it. A little girl visited the zoo one day. That night, she kneeled by her bed to say her prayers. "Dear God," she said, "did you mean to make the giraffe that way or was it an accident?"

She was amazed by the giraffe. If we, like children, take the time to really look at things, we too will be ceaselessly amazed. There is so much in life, nature, in people to give rise to amazement and wonder. Do you ever stop and contemplate the mystery of life? Do you take all the flowers and trees and creatures upon the earth for granted or are you awed by the wonder of it all? There is beauty in the world and in our minds.

We visited Vietnam during our world cruise. In a market in a back alley of a small village, I was taking pictures with my digital camera. When I turned the camera around and showed the pictures to the Vietnamese, they were astonished and screamed with delight. They called their friends, and with each picture I took and showed them, they screamed and laughed and grabbed each other with wonder and joy.

One of the ironies of life is that sometimes the people who have the least are the most easily delighted. The more we have, the more complacent we become, taking our beautiful home or car or good health and happy family for granted. Take the time to be amazed.

Take the time to be good to yourself. Charity starts at home —with you. Take time to relax and refresh yourself. Take the time to discover and pursue what you really enjoy. Take time to look good. Your appearance affects how you feel about yourself, and influences other people's opinion of you. Be kind to yourself, patient and forgiving. Take the lessons from your mistakes and let the self-recrimination go. Guilt is a poisonous emotion. It keeps you from feeling good about yourself, and how you feel about yourself affects the quality of your life, your relationships and everything you do.

Take the time to be kind. I still feel sad for the man who told me, "My wife died 7 years ago. I've adapted. I'm doing fine. The one thing that still bothers me is that I could have made her happier. My life was my job. My wife and kids, well, they were just there. She never complained. I think she was happy. But I could have made her happier. It would have taken so little and it would have been so nice for her. And for me."

Don't let those opportunities get away. Wherever you are, there is someone you can make a little happier. For years my mother used to quote a poem that had a line in it something like, "I want to sit by the side of the road and be a friend to mankind." She said that's what she wanted to do. Amazingly, that is what she ended up doing!

"There are a lot of people in here who don't have anyone to visit them," she told me one day. "So, I go to their door and I lean in and say, 'How are you doing today?' And they are so happy to have someone to talk to. I go in and they tell me everything."

Compassionate listening is an act of love, and a gift more precious than words. Take time to listen. Giving is depleting if done to get something in return. Giving out of the fullness of one's own being, giving because you're filled to overflowing with love and laughter and happiness and gratitude is restorative and rewarding.

Life flows to us as we let it flow through us. Open the gates of your being. Share your smiles and kind words with everyone. Take the advice of the 8 year old who said, "You really shouldn't say 'I love you' unless you mean it. But if you mean it, you should say it a lot. People forget."

Open your heart, your mind, your arms, your eyes. Most of us have built walls around ourselves. We are in a constant state of self-defense. We are afraid of being hurt, disappointed, betrayed, rejected. Our fears imprison us. Let the walls down.

> *So often time it happens, we all live our life in chains,*
> *and we never even know we have the key.*
> *— The Eagles*

Open your mind to new ideas. Open your heart to a pet, a child, a lonely neighbor. One lady I knew and loved was the epitome of unconditional love. She literally had an open door policy. Anyone could walk in any time, have a cup of tea or coffee, and talk about anything without fear of judgment. She was the best listener I ever knew. I doubt she ever heard this poem, but she certainly lived by it...

Lord, thou knowest I am growing old.

Keep me from becoming talkative and possessed with the idea that I must express myself on every subject.

Release me from the craving to straighten out everyone's affairs.

Keep me from the recital of endless detail. Give me wings to get to the point.

Seal my lips when I am inclined to tell of my aches and pains. They are increasing with the years and my love to speak of them grows sweeter as time goes by.

Teach me the glorious lesson that occasionally I may be wrong.

Make me thoughtful but not nosey; helpful but not bossy.

With my vast store of wisdom and experience it does seem a pity not to use it all.

But Thou knowest, Lord, that I want a few friends at the end.

Author unknown

* * * * * *

Life is a classroom and as we meet its challenges and grow, we gain wisdom and understanding. If we greet the years ahead with enthusiasm and anticipation, we will discover that they hold many gifts for us. I never expected to be writing this book. But then, previous to our world cruise, I never imagined lecturing on cruise ships. One thing leads to another, and then another. Life takes some exciting twists and turns if we let go of the wheel now and then and open ourselves to the myriad of possibilities available to each of us.

My thanks to Barbara, June and Ann for sharing their inspiring stories. I am grateful to all the people I've met on cruise ships who encouraged me to write this book and also took the time to share some of their stories. Ron, my husband, was extremely patient and supportive as I spent day after day working on this manuscript. He listened to every word and made some helpful suggestions for which I am most grateful. And, of course, my thanks to my mother whose love and inspiration are always with me.

I sincerely hope that this book has encouraged and inspired you, that your life will be more fulfilling because of the voyage we have taken together. As you disembark and go off to follow your own unique path, I hope you will be among the millions of people who are making the best of the rest of their life.

SUGGESTED READING: *The Power Of Now* by Eckhart Tolle

QUOTES TO LIVE BY:

Aldous Huxley said it was embarrassing to end his life and have nothing more profound to say than,
"Be a little kinder."

May God grant you always…

A sunbeam to warm you
A moonbeam to charm you
A sheltering angel
So nothing can harm you…

Laughter to cheer you
Faithful friends near you
And whenever you pray
Heaven to hear you.

Irish prayer